Men-at-Arms • 460

Frederick the Great's Allies 1756–63

Stuart Reid • Illustrated by Gerry & Sam Embleton

Series editor Martin Windrow

First published in Great Britain in 2010 by Osprey Publishing
Midland House, West Way, Botley, Oxford OX2 0PH, UK
44–02 23rd St, Suite 219, Long Island City, NY 11101, USA
E-mail: **info@ospreypublishing.com**

A CIP catalogue record for this book is available from the British Library

ISBN: 978 1 84908 177 1
ebook ISBN: 978 1 84908 178 8

Editor: Martin Windrow
Page layouts by Myriam Bell Design, France
Typeset in Helvetica Neue and ITC New Baskerville
Index by Fineline Editorial Services
Originated by United Graphics Pte Ltd.
Printed in China through World Print Ltd.

10 11 12 13 14   10 9 8 7 6 5 4 3 2 1

FOR A CATALOGUE OF ALL BOOKS PUBLISHED BY OSPREY MILITARY
AND AVIATION PLEASE CONTACT:

Osprey Direct, c/o Random House Distribution Center,
400 Hahn Road, Westminster, MD 21157
Email: uscustomerservice@ospreypublishing.com

Osprey Direct, The Book Service Ltd, Distribution Centre,
Colchester Road, Frating Green, Colchester, Essex, CO7 7DW
E-mail: customerservice@ospreypublishing.com

Osprey Publishing is supporting the Woodland Trust, the UK's leading
Woodland conservation charity, by funding the dedication of trees.

www.ospreypublishing.com

Artist's note

Readers may care to note that the original paintings from which
the colour plates in this book were prepared are available for
private sale. All reproduction copyright whatsoever is retained
by the Publishers. All enquiries should be addressed to:

www.gerryembleton.com

The Publishers regret that they can enter into no correspondence
upon this matter.

FREDERICK THE GREAT'S ALLIES 1756–1763

INTRODUCTION

Amore valid title for this study might actually be *His Britannic Majesty's Army in Germany*, for in reality Frederick II the Great of Prussia had very few allies during the Seven Years' War, and all of them were grouped together into a single army, largely in British pay. This was led at first by King George's son William Augustus, Duke of Cumberland, and subsequently by a Prussian general, the *Erzhog* Ferdinand of Brunswick.

The key to it all, however, was Hanover, whose monarchy was held simultaneously by King George II of England. As Elector of Hanover he was at peace with the world in 1756, but as King of England he was simultaneously engaged in a low-intensity war with France in the American colonies and in India.[1] When this conflict began to escalate, France decided to retaliate by threatening King George's vulnerable Electorate of Hanover. At that time a defensive alliance was still in force between France and Prussia, and it was tactfully suggested by the envoys of King Louis XV that if Frederick cared to invade Hanover, France would reciprocate by attacking his enemies in the Austrian Netherlands (modern Belgium). Hanover was all but defenceless, possessing no natural boundaries, and half her army was abroad protecting England against the illusory threat of French invasion. Nevertheless, Frederick, who had troubles enough of his own, declined this ingenious invitation, while kindly offering France the use of the Rhineland fortress of Wesel for any attempt she might care to make on her own account.

For his part, George II's prime minister William Pitt initially responded to this threat by concluding a not very secret alliance with Russia, promising the Empress Elizabeth I a substantial financial subsidy for launching a seaborne invasion of Prussia in the event of any Prussian attack on Hanover. Then, with this precaution in place, the British ambassador presented Frederick with a full copy of the Russian treaty – and an invitation to enter into a defensive alliance with

Frederick II the Great of Prussia (1713–86) was Ferdinand of Brunswick's brother-in-law, but also his superior, since Ferdinand was an officer of the Prussian army. Consequently, 'Old Fritz' was sometimes wont to treat Ferdinand as a subordinate rather than as the commander of an allied force.

1 See Men-at-Arms 48, *Wolfe's Army*; MAA 313, *Louis XV's Army (5) Colonial and Naval Troops*; MAA 453, *Armies of the East India Company 1750–1850*; Warrior 85, *American Colonial Ranger 1724–64*; WAR 126, *Highlander in the French-Indian War 1756–67*; and Campaign 121, *Quebec 1759*.

Britain and Hanover, in order to neutralize this 'Russian threat' and safeguard the Electorate... Although this was a particularly blatant piece of blackmail, Frederick readily assented to the proposal, which made far more strategic sense for Prussia than the existing alliance with France. Thus rebuffed, Louis XV proceeded instead to enter into a defensive alliance with the Holy Roman Empire (Austria), with whom she had been intermittently at war for the past 200 years and more.

With the old patterns of alliances completely turned on their heads, and with his western flank thus secured, Frederick of Prussia embarked upon an invasion of France's ally Saxony in August 1756, thus beginning the Seven Years' War.

William Augustus, Duke of Cumberland, was the Allied army's first commander, until dismissed by King George II after failing to secure a victory at the battle of Hastenbeck; he then obeyed his royal father's instructions to conclude a cease-fire.

CHRONOLOGY

1756:
16 Jan Britain and Prussia sign Convention of Westminster
1 May France and Austria (Empire) sign Treaty of Versailles
19 June Prussian mobilization begins
28 Aug Prussia invades Saxony, beginning the Seven Years' War

1757:
25 Mar French hussars exchange fire with garrison of Geldern
14 Apr Duke of Cumberland assumes command of Hanoverian Army
26 July After French and Imperialists invade Hanover, Cumberland is narrowly defeated by Marshal d'Estrées at Hastenbeck
10 Sept Armistice with French signed at Kloster Zeven
5 Nov (Prussians defeat French and Imperialists at Rossbach)
23 Nov Ferdinand of Brunswick assumes command of Allied army
26 Nov Allied breakout begins, leading to French withdrawal
5 Dec (Prussians defeat Imperialists at Leuthen)

1758:
12 June Allied victory at Krefeld
23 July French victory at Sandershausen
3 Aug First British contingent disembarks at Emden
10 Oct French victory at Lutterberg

1759:
13 Apr French victory at Bergen, near Frankfurt
1 Aug Allied victory at Minden
12 Aug (Russians and Imperialists defeat Prussians at Kunersdorf)

1760:
10 July French victory at Korbach
16 July Allied victory at Emsdorf
31 July Allied victory at Warburg
5 Sept Allied raid on Zierenberg

16 Oct	Allies checked at Kloster Kamp
25 Oct	(King George II of England is succeeded by George III, who will gradually abandon alliance, reducing subsidies to Prussia and withdrawing British troops)
3 Nov	(Prussians win costly victory at Torgau)

1761:

| 16 June | Allied victory at Vellinghausen |
| Oct | Allied army forced to retreat to Brunswick |

1762:

5 Jan	(Empress Elizabeth of Russia succeeded by Tsar Peter III, who opens peace negotiations with Prussia)
22 May	(Treaty of Hamburg – Sweden withdraws from anti-Prussian alliance)
24 June	Allied victory over French at Wilhelmsthal
9 July	(Empress Catherine II deposes Tsar Peter, but does not renew war with Prussia)
21 July	(Prussians defeat Imperialists at Burkersdorf)
23 July	Allied victory over French at Lutterberg
30 Aug	French victory over Allies at Nauheim
21 Sept	French capture Amoneburg
Oct/Nov	Allied army drives French back over Rhine
15 Nov	Armistice signed between Allied and French forces

1763:

| 16 Feb | With all belligerents exhausted, Treaty of Hubertusburg between Prussia and Holy Roman Empire finally ends Seven Years' War |

HIS BRITANNIC MAJESTY'S ARMY IN GERMANY

The largest part of the army was its Hanoverian contingent, which comprised not only the entirety of the Hanoverian army proper, but also included small subsidiary contingents from the neighbouring states of Sachsen-Gotha and Buckeburg; these were directly in Hanoverian pay, and were ultimately absorbed into the Hanoverian army. Excluding those contingents, at the outbreak of war the Hanoverian army had an establishment of some 29,000 men, mustering 34 squadrons of cavalry, 29 battalions of infantry and 8 companies of artillery. Light troops amounted to just one company of hussars and six of Jägers. During the course of the war the establishment of regular troops was increased only slightly, but the light troops would expand more than four-fold.

Next in order of importance came the armies of Hesse-Kassel (not to be confused with Hesse-Darmstadt) and Brunswick, which were not allied contingents in a political sense but were directly

An impression of a battle of the Seven Years' War, with Prussian infantry in the foreground drawn up behind *chevaux-de-frise* field defences.

Ferdinand of Brunswick (1721–92), commander of the Allied army from November 1757. This portrait by Johan Georg Zeisnis depicts him in the uniform of an officer of the Prussian Infanterie-Regiment Nr.39, adorned with the star of the British Order of the Garter awarded for the victory at Minden.

leased by the British government. Initially the Hessian contingent accounted for 16 cavalry squadrons, 14 infantry battalions and two artillery companies; the Brunswick contingent originally comprised just one cavalry and four infantry regiments, totalling two squadrons and 10 battalions. There was also, from 1758, a strong British contingent, and a small Prussian force was incorporated into the Allied army.

At the outset this rather heterogeneous army was placed under the command of King George's son William Augustus, Duke of Cumberland. This prince of the blood, best known in Britain for his Culloden campaign, was also a Hanoverian general officer; he had experience of commanding a multi-national force in Flanders during the previous War of the Austrian Succession, and was considered the best possible choice. Unfortunately, he got off to a bad start: he had insufficient troops, and official instructions that specifically defined his primary role as the defence of Hanover, forbidding him from interfering should the French by-pass the Electorate in order to join with the Imperialist forces in Bohemia. Consequently, when a replacement was required after the botched battle of Hastenbeck in July and Cumberland's subsequent armistice at Kloster Zeven in September 1757, Frederick was only too keen to allow his brother-in-law, Ferdinand of Brunswick, to take over command.

This appointment was at first welcomed by George II, but later regretted, when it became clear that Ferdinand (unsurprisingly) regarded co-operation with Frederick to be a higher priority than the defence of Hanover. Nevertheless, under Ferdinand's command the

The battle of Minden, 1 August 1759 (see Plate E). This spirited illustration by Harry Payne of the advance of the British infantry contingent in Gen von Spörcken's division is slightly marred by the prominence of the grenadiers, who were actually detached to form a consolidated battalion that was serving under Gen von Wangenheim on a different part of the battlefield.

Allied army developed into an efficient fighting machine, which for much of the war secured Frederick's vulnerable western flank against the French and left him free to concentrate on his many other enemies to the north, east and south. In the process it produced one of the British Army's most famous battle honours in its 'Year of Victories'– Minden, 1759.

ORGANIZATION AND UNIFORMS: CAVALRY

The mounted element of the Allied army can essentially be divided between 'battle cavalry' – variously designated as Kürassier, Karabinier, Cavallerie, Reiter, Horse or Dragoons; and hussars, who are separately described in this text under the heading 'Light Troops' (below).

At the outset, Ferdinand does not appear to have been particularly impressed by his battle cavalry, who seemingly manoeuvred slowly, and demonstrated a distinct preference for shooting it out with carbines rather than relying on swift movement in the Prussian style. This may seem surprising, since the superiority of shock tactics had been repeatedly demonstrated since the early 17th century; yet time and again cavalry had manifested a reliance on firearms rather than charging home with the sword. This was not a question of clinging to outmoded doctrines, but was rather due to a lack of peacetime training at any level above that of the single troop of horse. Armies suffered from the absence of any real opportunities to practice cavalry manoeuvres at regimental level, let alone in brigades or larger formations. Consequently, when they were called upon to do so in wartime there was an understandable tendency to move more slowly than necessary in order to preserve the dressing of the formations, as prescribed in the drill-book. (Indeed, it was testified at the court-martial of Lord Sackville after Minden that he 'always marched slow' for precisely that reason.) Thus, by default rather than by design, too much reliance came to be placed on the use of firearms.

With this tendency in mind, Ferdinand therefore begged and received from Frederick a brigade of Prussian dragoons, not just as a reinforcement but primarily in order to serve as an exemplar to teach his own cavalry how to speed up their movements and make proper use of shock action – which they soon did, with splendid results.

BRUNSWICK CAVALRY

Brunswick possessed a single regular cavalry regiment. Originally it was a dragoon unit, mustering four companies each of three officers and 66 men. This regiment was not included in the

Hanoverian mounted grenadier, Grenadieren zu Pferde, by Richard Knötel (see Plate B1). The mitre cap has a black front bearing the arms of Hanover, with a red 'little flap' bearing the white horse badge; the colours are reversed on the rear, with a red 'bag' piped in yellow above a black headband, and a red/black tuft on top. The red coat has red turnbacks, and black cuffs and lapels edged yellow; waistcoat, breeches and leather belts are buff. Note the slung musket, its butt held by a 'boot' on the nearside of the saddle below the holster housing. The horse furniture is red with King George's 'GR' cypher within a crowned garter, and black-and-yellow edging.

Lord George Sackville (1716–85). This engraving after Reynolds depicts him wearing an interesting fur-trimmed Hungarian-style coat – an entirely non-regulation garment typical of the latitude allowed in senior officers' dress. Commander of the British contingent until unfairly scapegoated by Ferdinand for his own command failings at Minden, Sackville was forced to resign his commission, but was effectively acquitted at his later court-martial.

original contract for Allied service, but in 1759 it was added to the subsidiary contingent. It was also enlarged before joining the army, converting to Karabiniere status and being increased to six companies totalling 502 officers and men, organized in three squadrons.

The original uniform is depicted in our Plate G3, but upon becoming carabiniers an entirely new uniform closely resembling that of Prussian cuirassiers was adopted instead. This comprised a buff-coloured *Kollet* with red cuffs and trim – a short, single-breasted coat fastened with hooks rather than buttons, which had evolved from the thick buff-leather coats worn by 17th century cavalrymen – with a red sash and sabretache, and a black cuirass. (The change in status was evidently expensive, and in 1772 the regiment would revert once again to being dragoons, adopting a Prussian-style uniform with sky-blue coats faced yellow.)

BRITISH CAVALRY

From the outset of the alliance Frederick of Prussia had requested that some British cavalry be sent to Germany. The request was made in hope rather than expectation, but to his delight six cavalry regiments totalling 14 squadrons landed with the first contingent in August 1758, and another 14 squadrons at various dates between May and July 1760, for a total of 28 squadrons (exclusive of the three-squadron 15th Light Dragoons, described here under 'Light Troops').

Like their continental counterparts, the British cavalry comprised regiments designated as both Horse and Dragoons. Since 1746 a number of the former had been redesignated as Dragoon Guards as an economy measure, but in practical terms this terminological alteration made no real difference. Their basic organization was similar to that of the Hanoverian cavalry, with six companies (designated as 'troops') in each regiment, grouped into two squadrons; however, two of the regiments serving in Germany – the Royal Horse Guards and the 1st Dragoon Guards – had nine troops apiece, grouped in three squadrons. In 1756 an additional 'light' troop was added to all but the Horse Guards, but it is unclear whether these actually served in Germany.

British cavalry uniforms were different from their German counterparts in two important regards. In the first place, with the exception of the Royal Horse Guards ('the Blues'), all wore red coats in conformity with their infantry comrades, rather than a contrasting colour. Secondly, in German armies it was usually the case that dragoons were distinguished from heavier cavalry by the addition of contrasting-coloured lapels on their coats. In the British service this convention was reversed, with regiments of Horse having fairly narrow full-length lapels on their coats, while Dragoon Guards had infantry-style half-lapels, and Dragoons wore double-breasted coats (normally worn open over waistcoats) without lapels.

Facing colours were displayed on cuffs, lapels and turnbacks, and also in waistcoats and breeches. None of the regiments had lace edge-binding to the lapels or cuffs; otherwise the usual conventions were observed, with button-loops, hat lace and, in the case of Dragoons, the aiguillettes on the right shoulder all corresponding to the button colour (i.e. white/silver or yellow/gold). There is no evidence that any of the Dragoon regiments still maintained grenadier companies wearing mitre caps at this period, but all ranks of the 2nd Royal North British Dragoons did so, at least for guard mountings and formal parades.

Equipment was of buff leather with the exception of the 2nd RNB Dragoons, who whitened their belts (although it seems likely that other regiments followed this trend over time, since it was confirmed in the 1764 Warrant). The Blues and regiments of Horse and Dragoon Guards carried their swords on a baldric slung over the right shoulder, crossed with the usual carbine belt slung over the left shoulder; a decorative flask cord in the facing colour was attached to the centre of the latter. Dragoon regiments carried their swords (and bayonets) frogged from a belt around the waist, and had an infantry-style cartridge box on a sling over the left shoulder.

Both types of cavalry were equipped with broadswords with basket hilts of regimental pattern, and carbines. Those carried by Dragoons were in effect slightly shortened infantry muskets, and were easily distinguished from those carried by Horse and Dragoon Guards by the fact that the latter, although only very slightly shorter, were fully stocked to the muzzle and could not be fitted with a bayonet.

Horse furniture was to be of the same colour as the facings, except in the 1st King's Dragoon Guards and 1st Royal Dragoons, which both

British officer's grenadier-style cap of the 2nd (Royal North British) Dragoons. Blue front bearing Garter star with white centre and red cross, and silver decoration; the 'little flap' is red with the thistle device in silver.

Hanoverian cavalry, by Richard Knötel:
LEFT **Kürassiere-Regiment von Hammerstein. Plain black hat with oakleaf field sign. White coat with black cuffs and turnbacks; buff waistcoat and breeches; buff leather belts. Horse furniture black, edged red-and-white; 'GR' on red cartouches surrounded by crowned garter, within red and white wreaths.**

RIGHT **Kürassiere-Regiment Dachenhausen. White coat with apple-green cuffs and turnbacks; buff waistcoat and breeches; buff carbine belt. Horse furniture apple-green with red 'GR' cartouches, red and white crowns and wreaths.**

Knötel illustrations of Hanoverian dragoons:

LEFT **Dragoner-Regiment von Bussche. One company of each dragoon regiment was designated as grenadiers and accordingly wore a mitre cap rather than the usual tricorne, in this case of dark blue cloth with yellow trim. White coat with blue cuffs, lapels and turnbacks, yellow metal buttons. Buff waistcoat and breeches; buff leather equipment – note grenadier's brass matchcase on cartridge box sling. Horse furniture is blue – see text for this unit's complex edging arrangement.**

RIGHT **Dragoner-Regiment von Dachenhausen. White coat with red cuffs, lapels and turnbacks, and red cords on right shoulder; white lace edging to cuffs and lapels, and white lace button-loops. Buff waistcoat and breeches, buff leather belts. Horse furniture red, edged white-and-black; white horse of Hanover surrounded by white wreath surmounted by crown.**

had red, and the 4th Horse, with buff-coloured furniture. Items were edged with yellow worsted or mohair (white) lace with a stripe in the middle; this was dark blue for Royal regiments, including those designated as King's or Queen's regiments irrespective of their facing colour. These and other titled regiments also had an appropriate badge or device on the housings – for instance, the castle for the Inniskillings; ordinary regiments had to be content with their number in Roman numerals upon a red cartouche, while all displayed the royal cypher 'GR' on the holster covers.

Regimental distinctions:
(* Units marked thus landed with the first British contingent in 1758.)
*Royal Horse Guards** Blue coats faced red; red waistcoat and breeches; brass buttons, gold lace on hat
*1st King's Dragoon Guards** Blue facings; yellow lace with button-loops set in pairs; gold hat-lace
2nd Queen's Dragoon Guards Buff facings with half-lapels; yellow lace with loops set three and three
*3rd Dragoon Guards** White facings with half-lapels; yellow lace with loops set in pairs
2nd Horse Green facings with full lapels; yellow lace with loops set in pairs
3rd Horse (Carabiniers) Pale yellow facings with full lapels; white lace with loops set in pairs
4th Horse Black cuffs and full lapels; buff turnbacks, waistcoats and breeches; yellow lace with loops set in pairs
1st Royal Dragoons Blue facings; yellow lace with loops set in pairs
*2nd Royal North British Dragoons** Blue facings; white lace with loops set in pairs. This unit had a number of peculiarities: in addition to their grenadier caps, they were distinguished by riding grey horses (and their eccentric commanding officer, Col Preston, insisted on wearing an old-fashioned buff coat in action)

*6th Inniskilling Dragoons** Full yellow facings; white lace with loops set in pairs (see Plate E3)

7th Queen's Dragoons White facings and lace, with loops set three and three

*10th Dragoons** Deep yellow facings; white lace with loops set three, four and five

11th Dragoons Buff facings; white lace with loops set three and three

HANOVERIAN CAVALRY

The **Guard cavalry** comprised one regiment designated as Garde du Corps, with three companies forming a single squadron, and mustering at the outset a total of only 188 officers and men. A second regiment was designated as Grenadieren zu Pferde (Horse Grenadiers), and while organized in two companies rather than three it had a near identical establishment of 187 officers and men.

Both regiments wore red coats, with straw-coloured waistcoats and breeches. The Garde du Corps were distinguished by red cuffs, dark blue turnbacks and silver lace; the Grenadieren zu Pferde had black cuffs and lapels, red turnbacks, and cloth mitre caps in place of cocked hats. These had black fronts bearing the arms of Hanover in gold with gold scrollwork; the frontal 'little flap' was red, with the white horse of Hanover and the motto *Nec Aspera Terram* in white. The rear of the cap was in reversed colours, the main 'bag' part being red piped in gold, with a black headband embellished with gold grenades.

As quasi-dragoons the Grenadieren zu Pferde carried infantry-style cartridge boxes on the right hip and belts in buff leather, and a 'booted' musket (i.e. slung from the shoulder, with its butt held in a pocket or 'boot' strapped to the saddle in front of the right leg), in place of the carbine hooked to a crossbelt, as issued to cavalry regiments proper such as the Garde du Corps. Both regiments had red saddle housings (horse furniture), bordered in silver for the Garde du Corps and in yellow and black for the Grenadieren zu Pferde. One source states that the former were mounted on grey horses.

The **Line cavalry** were similarly divided, between cuirassiers and dragoons; the principal difference between the two was in internal organization. The Leib-Regiment ('body[guard] regiment') and seven regiments of Kürassiere each comprised six companies, formed into two squadrons, with a total establishment of 361 officers and men. The four dragoon regiments were considerably larger, each having eight companies organized in four squadrons, with a total of 715 all ranks.

All cavalry regiments wore white coats with facing-coloured collar, cuffs and turnbacks; straw-coloured 'smallclothes' (waistcoats and breeches); and either tin or brass buttons matching their hat-lace colour. Notwithstanding

Hessian Leib-Dragoner, by Knötel. The red facings on the blue coat brought this regiment the name of '*der Rote Dragoner*', distinguishing them from the other Hessian dragoon regiment, which had yellow facings.

Hesse-Kassel cavalrymen, by Knötel:

LEFT **Kürassiere-Regiment von Miltitz.** White coat and breeches, dark blue collar and cuffs; gold lace on coat and hat; white belts. Horse furniture dark blue with gold lace.

RIGHT **Dragoner-Regiment von Dittfurth.** White hat-lace. White coat (other sources give light blue) with yellow collar, cuffs, turnbacks and lapels; straw-coloured waistcoat and breeches. Yellow horse furniture edged white.

their designation, none of the cuirassiers actually wore armour at this period. Dragoons differed in having facing-coloured lapels on the front of the coat, and their original status as mounted infantry was also marked by one of the eight companies being designated as grenadiers, distinguished by wearing mitre caps. Equipment comprised buff belts, a steel-hilted sword, a pair of pistols in saddle-holsters and a carbine. Like the Grenadieren zu Pferde, dragoons carried infantry-style cartridge boxes, belts in buff leather, and a 'booted' musket in place of the carbine and belt issued to cavalry regiments.

Regimental numbers were not allocated until the post-war re-organization; as was customary in most armies, each unit was instead referred to solely by the name of its current *Inhaber* or colonel-proprietor. (However, for the avoidance of confusion, in this text all regiments in the Hanoverian, Hessian and Brunswick armies are referred to by the name of their 1756 Inhaber.)

Regimental distinctions – Cuirassiers
Leib-Regiment Yellow facings and lace; white/red hat pompons. Yellow saddle housings, red edging with black half-circles; device of cypher within crowned garter, with white and red scrollwork
Skolln Orange facings, yellow lace, white pompons. Orange housings edged with two bands of light blue with a double zig-zag in yellow; white horse badge within crowned garter, no scrollwork
Dachenhausen Light green facings, white lace, white pompons. Light green housings edged with yellow/white/red scroll pattern; white horse within crowned garter
Hammerstein Dark green facings, yellow lace, green/white pompons. Dark green housings, with a border of yellow and white rectangles edged in red; cypher within crowned garter, with red, yellow and white scrollwork

Grothaus Crimson facings, yellow lace, silver pompons. Crimson housings, edged with white spiral scroll edged yellow between two yellow stripes; white horse within crowned garter, yellow and white scrollwork

Hodenburg Scarlet facings, white lace, blue pompons. Scarlet housings edged with border of three stripes of red and black diagonals edged yellow; cypher within crowned garter, white and yellow scrollwork

Walthausen Dark blue facings, yellow lace, blue pompons. Dark blue housings edged with white and yellow diagonals; white horse within crowned garter; red, white and yellow scrollwork

Gilten Sky-blue facings, white lace, white pompons. Sky-blue housings, with broad red border edged yellow/blue/yellow; white horse within crowned garter, no scrollwork.

Regimental distinctions – Dragoons

Dachenhausen Red facings, white lace, white pompons. Red housings with border of the same edged white and black; white horse within crowned black and white scrollwork

Breidenbach Light blue facings, white lace, white pompons. Light blue housings with narrow outer edge of one red stripe on white, and an inner border of two red stripes on white; white horse within crowned garter, white scrollwork

Bussche Bright blue facings, yellow lace, white pompons. Bright blue housings with outer border of white edged yellow with blue zig-zag, and inner border of red edged yellow, with white scroll intertwining a white central stripe; white horse within crowned white scrollwork

Bock Scarlet facings, yellow lace, white pompons. Scarlet housings, yellow border bearing pattern of red diamonds with blue centres, edged first with blue, and then on either side a red stripe edged with white with a white zig-zag. Device of white horse within crowned garter placed entirely within unusually broad border.

HESSIAN CAVALRY

As usual, the Hesse-Kassel cavalry were divided between Horse – in this case designated as Reiters – and Dragoons, with the former accounting for eight squadrons paired into four regiments, while the latter comprised two larger regiments each of four squadrons. Following the accession of the *Landgraf* Frederick II in 1760, a dramatic but ultimately insubstantial reorganization of the army took place. The *Landgraf* himself had served (with scant distinction) in the Prussian army, and immediately set about remodelling his own in the Prussian image. In the case of the cavalry a small Garde du Corps was added to the establishment, though apparently serving only in a ceremonial role. The four Reiter regiments were redesignated as Kürassiere, duly exchanging their white frock coats for buff-coloured Prussian-style *Kollets,* with facing-coloured sashes

Prussian Dragoner-Regiment Nr.9, as depicted in Knötel's *Uniformenkunde*. This regiment earned a good reputation while serving with the Allied army in the brigade commanded by the Duke of Holstein-Gottorp. See Plate B3 for uniform details; the edging of the horse furniture is white with two red lines, and note the long picket-stake carried strapped to the carbine by Prussian dragoons.

supporting waist-level sabretaches. They should also have received black cuirasses, but there seems to be some doubt as to whether these were actually issued.

Regimental distinctions

Leib-Regiment Initially, white coats with red collars, cuffs, lapels and turnbacks; buff waistcoats and breeches, and brass buttons. Pompons, appearing at the sides of the hat but not at the front, were plain red. In 1760 the regiment was redesignated *Gensdarmes* and given buff-coloured Kollets, again with red collar and cuffs, and red waistcoats.

Reiter-Regiment Wilhelm Same uniform but with dark blue facings; this unit became the *Kurrasiere-Regiment Erbprinz* in 1760

Reiter-Regiment Militiz Similarly dressed but with green facings; (1760) became *Kurassiere-Regiment Einsidel*

Reiter-Regiment Pruschek Light blue facings, and differed from the others in having tin rather than brass buttons. (1760) became *Kurrasiere-Regiment Wolff*

For all four regiments the saddle housings were of the facing colour, with two bands of yellow or white edging according to button colour.

Unsurprisingly, the uniform of the two Hessian Dragoon regiments was patterned after that of the Prussian army. David Morier in 1748 (and Richard Knötel following him) depicts the coat as being fairly dark blue in colour, but it is possible that this was altered to Prussian sky-blue under the 1760 reforms. Both units had buff-coloured waistcoats and breeches, and whitened leather equipment. As with the other cavalry units, horse furniture was facing-coloured, edged with two bands of lace.

Leib-Regiment ('*Rote Dragoner*') Red collars, cuffs, lapels and turnbacks; yellow hat lace; yellow aiguillette on right shoulder

Dragoner-Regiment Prinz Friedrich Yellow facings, white lace and cords

PRUSSIAN CAVALRY

Early in 1758 Ferdinand of Brunswick was reinforced by a small brigade of 15 squadrons of Prussian regular cavalry commanded by Duke George Ludwig of Holstein-Gottorp. Ten of these squadrons were dragoons, belonging to Regiment Nr.9 (Holstein-Gottorp) and Regiment Nr.10 (Finckenstein). The other five squadrons were hussars (see under 'Light Troops', below).

The experiment was successful; each in their own ways, Holstein-Gottorp's dragoons and hussars proved extremely effective, and their example went a long way to increasing the overall efficiency of the other Allied cavalry. Unfortunately, Frederick the Great soon began demanding their return as he himself came under ever greater pressure from the Imperialists and Russians. Ferdinand was extremely reluctant to lose their services, and prevaricated to the point of insubordination before eventually releasing the dragoons in 1760, but the hussars remained under his command until the end of the war.

Both dragoon regiments wore sky-blue coats; Nr.9 had sky-blue collars, cuffs, and turnbacks, and Nr.10 wore orange facings. Neither regiment had lapels, but both wore a white aiguillette – i.e. a knot of cords in the button colour – attached behind the right shoulder. Waistcoats and breeches for both were straw-coloured, and horse furniture was facing-coloured.

INFANTRY

With the exception of the Hesse-Kassel contingent, discussed below, infantry regiments normally comprised single battalions, from which the grenadier companies were detached to serve in composite grenadier battalions. Initially these were used simply as additional battalions on the field of battle; but as the war went on they were increasingly detached for employment in *Kleinkrieg* ('little war') operations, to stiffen the rather dubious materials making up the various 'free corps' also entrusted with such missions.

Infantry tactics went through a process of change under the leadership of Ferdinand of Brunswick. At the outset of the war the 'platoon-firing' system was in favour; battalions were drawn up in three ranks and arbitrarily told off into lateral platoons, which then fired in a pre-arranged sequence intended to maintain a continuous rolling fire. As with the prevailing cavalry tactics, this tended to be a rather ponderous business, requiring a degree of training not always attainable under wartime conditions. Accordingly Ferdinand introduced the much simpler Prussian 'alternate-firing' system, under which companies were paired off to fire alternately in their own time. The same system had also been introduced (albeit unofficially) to the British Army by James Wolfe, and the integration of British and German infantry was consequently a good deal smoother than the parallel integration of the first cavalry contingent.

BRUNSWICK INFANTRY

Brunswick infantry regiments each consisted of five 'musketeer' (*Musketier*) companies and one grenadier company. On paper the total establishment of each regiment was 1,470 officers and men, but aside from the usual attritional problems each unit was weakened in wartime by the permanent detachment of the grenadier companies to form the consolidated grenadier battalions.

Knötel illustrations of Brunswick infantry:
LEFT **Drummer of the Leib-Regiment. Silver scalloped lace on hat with red pompons. Yellow coat with red collar, cuffs, turnbacks, and swallow's-nests, with silver lace; white waistcoat and breeches. White drum-sling, black apron; brass-fronted drum, white cords; red bands decorated with black diagonals edged yellow.**

RIGHT **Officer of Infanterie-Regiment von Imhoff – see Plate G2 for uniform detail.**

The four infantry regiments were very Prussian in appearance, with dark blue coats, white waistcoats and breeches, and black gaiters; musketeers had white-laced hats irrespective of the regimental button colour.

Regimental distinctions
Leib-Regiment No lapels, red cuffs and turnbacks; scalloped lace on hats; brass grenadier cap plates with dark blue 'bag' and red band at the rear; plain red pompons
Regiment von Behr Red cuffs, turnbacks and lapels; plain hat-lace; tin cap plates; red-and-white pompons
Regiment von Imhoff (see Plate G3) White distinctions; brass cap plates; blue-and-white pompons
Regiment von Zastrow Yellow distinctions; tin cap plates; white-and-yellow pompons

The two grenadier battalions were formed by pairing the companies from the Leib-Regiment and Imhoff, and those from Behr and Zastrow. As in the Hanoverian army, both battalions became independent of their parent regiments in 1759. The first was simply redesignated as Grenadiere-Bataillon von Stammer. The second was divided, with the company from Behr forming the cadre of Grenadiere-Bataillon von Redecken and that from Zastrow providing the backbone for Grenadiere-Bataillon von Wittdorf. The additional companies required to bring each up to strength were found from the militia, and presumably adopted the uniforms of the cadres.

(In addition to the regiments serving with Ferdinand's Allied army, a Leib-Grenadiere Garde and a Fusilier-Bataillon von Volschen were formed in 1759 and 1760 respectively, for home service, with the intention of stiffening the militia. Details are unrecorded, but the former were

Three battalions of British Footguards formed part of the 'Glorious Reinforcement' in 1759, serving in a brigade under MajGen Julius Caesar; as usual, the grenadier companies were consolidated into a separate battalion. David Morier's near-contemporary painting of a grenadier of each of the three regiments – part of a regimental series commissioned by the Duke of Cumberland in *c*.1751 – is an important source for general grenadier distinctions; see also Plate E2. Note the details of the cap, the broad cartridge-box sling with brass matchcase, and the narrower waist belt for the frogged bayonet and 'hanger'. Just visible behind the right shoulder of the right-hand grenadier, of the 3rd Footguards, is a corporal's shoulder-knot of white cords. For formal duties these soldiers wear white gaiters, with 36 black buttons; in the field black, brown or grey gaiters were substituted. (Reproduced by gracious permission of HM the Queen)

presumably dressed similarly to the Leib-Regiment with all wearing grenadier caps, while the latter probably had Prussian-style fusilier caps.)

BRITISH INFANTRY

All regiments comprised single battalions each of nine companies, one of which was designated as grenadiers and invariably detached to form composite grenadier battalions. All wore red coats, displaying the facing colour on cuffs, half-lapels and turnbacks. Coats were embellished with cuff and lapel edging and button-loops of white lace woven or embroidered with a unique regimental coloured pattern, although it was not unusual for this lace to be stripped off on service. Waistcoats were red irrespective of facing colour, as, normally, were the breeches; in theory Footguard battalions and Royal regiments were allowed blue breeches, but red ones were frequently observed. There was also a growing tendency, documented in paintings during this period, for officers to adopt buff-coloured waistcoats and breeches, and – perhaps as result of campaigning alongside German units – for the rank-and-file to adopt buff or straw-coloured breeches instead of red. Grenadiers wore cloth mitre caps, with fronts in the regimental facing colour and usually bearing the 'GR' cypher, though occasionally a regimental 'ancient badge'.

Col Robert Monckton did not serve in Germany, but his portrait provides a good example of the style of gold-laced scarlet uniform favoured by senior British officers at this time.

Regimental distinctions

(* Units marked thus landed with the first British contingent in 1758.)
1st Footguards Dark blue facings, button-loops set singly; Garter star on grenadier cap
2nd Footguards Dark blue facings, button-loops in pairs; Garter star on cap
3rd Footguards Dark blue facings, button-loops in threes; Thistle star on cap
5th Foot 'Gosling-green' facings; St George and Dragon on cap. (All ranks adopted fur grenadier caps in 1761, having captured them from the Grenadiers de France at Wilhelmstahl)
8th Foot Dark blue facings; white horse within crowned Garter on grenadier cap
11th Foot Green facings; 'GR' cypher on cap
*12th Foot** Yellow facings; 'GR' cypher
*20th Foot** Yellow facings; 'GR' cypher
*23rd Foot** Dark blue facings; Fusiliers – all ranks and companies wore caps with Prince of Wales's badge of three white feathers
24th Foot Light green facings; 'GR' cypher on grenadier cap
*25th Foot** Yellow facings; 'GR' cypher (see Plate E2)
33rd Foot Red facings; 'GR' cypher
*37th Foot** Yellow facings; 'GR' cypher
50th Foot Black facings; 'GR' cypher
*51st Foot** Dark green facings (see Plate E1); 'GR' cypher

HANOVERIAN INFANTRY

Aside from the Fussgarde, which boasted two battalions, Hanoverian infantry regiments each comprised a single battalion of seven companies, with an authorized establishment of 122 officers and men in each company, and a regimental staff of 19 (the Fussgarde had 20 staff, covering both battalions). Each company included (administratively) eight grenadiers, who were detached to provide the personnel for a composite company; this was itself assigned to one of three consolidated grenadier battalions for the duration of the campaign (except in the case of the Fussgarde, whose grenadiers were permanently assigned to protect Ferdinand of Brunswick's headquarters). The initial establishment of 29 battalions thus consisted of two Fussgarde battalions, 24 musketeer battalions and three grenadier battalions. Two further musketeer battalions were subsequently raised in 1758, with only five companies apiece and apparently without grenadiers.

A notional increase of a different sort was the decision to take a number of composite grenadier battalions into the line as units in their own right. Grenadier battalions were always regarded as a drain on their parent units, because the nature of their duties resulted in a higher degree of attrition than normal; these casualties then had to be made good by taking drafts from the musketeer companies, which in consequence sometimes dwindled alarmingly. Turning the consolidated grenadier battalions into permanent formations did not therefore increase the actual establishment of the army, but compelled the grenadiers to maintain themselves by regular recruitment rather than by simply milking the musketeer units.

All regiments wore red coats, with regimentally-coloured facings and (usually) waistcoats, and straw-coloured breeches. The grenadiers' cloth mitre caps had facing-coloured fronts and red 'bags'. As with the cavalry, regimental numbers were not allocated until the post-war re-organization, and until then units were referred to by the name of the current Inhaber; those listed below are the designations in 1757.

Regimental distinctions

Fussgarde Dark blue facings, yellow lace; white/yellow hat pompons
Scheither Dark green facings, yellow lace; green/yellow pompons
Alt-Zastrow White facings, yellow lace; red/yellow pompons
Spörcken Straw-coloured facings, yellow lace; red/yellow pompons
Fabrice Straw-coloured facings, white lace; straw/red pompons
Knesebeck Black cuffs and lapels, white lace; white waistcoats and turnbacks; red/black/white pompons
Druchtleben Black cuffs and lapels, yellow lace; yellow waistcoats and turnbacks; black/red pompons
Ledebour Medium blue facings, white lace; red/blue/white pompons
Stolzenberg Black cuffs and lapels, red turnbacks, white lace; straw-coloured waistcoats; yellow/white pompons
Grote Deep yellow facings, white lace; red/yellow/white pompons
Hodenberg Orange or straw-coloured facings, yellow lace; yellow pompons
Hardenberg Orange facings, white lace; red/yellow pompons
Caraffa Yellow facings, white lace; yellow/red pompons
Wangenheim Straw-coloured facings, white lace; straw-coloured pompons

British infantryman of c.1760 on the march, after a contemporary watercolour sketch by Paul or Thomas Sandby. Note the shorter gaiters with a stiffened knee-piece, and the very large weather-flap of the cartridge box, which was by now enlarged to take 35 rounds. The original sketch clearly suggests that he is wearing straw-coloured breeches rather than the regulation red.

Hauss Straw-coloured facings, yellow lace; straw/red pompons
Diepenbroick White facings and lace; red/white pompons
Block White facings and lace; red/white pompons
Sachsen-Gotha Green facings, white lace; green/red pompons. (Until absorbed into Hanoverian army in 1759, white coat faced green – see Plate A3)
Jung-Zastrow Dark green facings, white lace; dark green/white pompons
Post Green facings, white lace; white turnbacks and waistcoats; red/green/white pompons
Marschalk Red facings, white turnbacks and waistcoats, white lace
De Cheusses Yellow facings, yellow lace; straw-coloured turnbacks and waistcoats; red/yellow pompons
De La Chevallerie Yellow facings and lace; yellow/red pompons
Kielmansegge Light green facings, white lace; green/white pompons
Brunck Red facings and waistcoat, white turnbacks; white lace on hat only, green/white pompons
Halberstadt Blue facings, white lace; blue/red pompons
Wrede Red facings, white turnbacks and waistcoats; white lace on hat only, white/red pompons

HESSIAN INFANTRY

At the outset of the war the Hesse-Kassel infantry regiments each comprised one battalion of ten companies, but, as with the cavalry, a substantial reorganization took place in 1760. Thereafter the existing ten musketeer companies were consolidated into eight, and then divided into two battalions each of four companies. At the same time the practice of drawing eight men from each company to serve as grenadiers ceased, and instead the two remaining companies from each regiment were designated as grenadiers and detached to form consolidated battalions.

The 1760 reforms also brought about some confusing retitling. In 1757 the senior infantry regiment was promiscuously referred to as the

Knötel illustrations of Hanoverian infantry:

LEFT **Officer of the Fussgarde. Gold hat-lace, oakleaf field sign. Scarlet coat with dark blue cuffs, lapels and lining; gold lace cuff-edging and button-loops on coat. Unlaced dark blue waistcoat with gilt buttons. Buff or straw-coloured breeches; buff belt, gold shoulder-sash.**

CENTRE ***Unteroffizier*, Infanterie-Regiment Alt-Scheele. Silver hat-lace and pompon. Red coat with straw-coloured cuffs, lapels and turnbacks, and straw-coloured waistcoat, all edged with silver lace; silver lace button-loops. Buff breeches and belt.**

RIGHT **Grenadiers, Infanterie-Regiment von Scheither. Cap with dark green front, 'GR' on red cartouche within crowned garter; red 'little flap', white horse of Hanover; red rear 'bag', green band, all piped in yellow; red-and-green tuft. Red coat with dark green cuffs, lapels and turnbacks; yellow lace button-loops; unlaced dark green waistcoat. Buff breeches and belts.**

Uniforms of three Hanoverian Line regiments, by Knötel: LEFT *Fahnen-junker* (standard bearer) of Infanterie-Regiment von Hardenberg – see also Plate A2. Red coat with orange cuffs, lapels and turnbacks; silver lace edging to cuffs and lapels and on hat. Orange waistcoat trimmed with silver, and pale straw-coloured breeches.

CENTRE **Infanterie-Regiment von Knesebeck.** Black cuffs and lapels, white lace button-loops; white turnbacks and waistcoat; buff-coloured breeches; buff leather belts and gaiter-straps.

RIGHT **Infanterie-Regiment Alt-Zastrow.** Yellow hat-lace and red pompons. Red coat, white cuffs, lapels and turnbacks, yellow lace button-loops; white waistcoat; buff breeches; buff leather belts.

Garde or Leibgarde zu Fuss, while Infanterie-Regiment Nr.5 was the Leib-Regiment. However, in 1760 an entirely new guard battalion was raised and designated 1. Bataillon Garde; a consolidated grenadier battalion previously ranked sixth in seniority became 2. Garde; and the original Leibgarde found itself redesignated 3. Garde, both of the latter two being divided into two battalions. To further complicate matters the Regiment Erbprinz, formerly seventh in seniority, was first elevated to become 4. Garde, and then almost at once retitled Leib-Regiment; the former Leib-Regiment now became Infanterie-Regiment Wutginau; and the old Infanterie-Regiment Nr.12 became Erbprinz. Two regiments were also redesignated as fusiliers, probably because the Landgraf himself had commanded a fusilier regiment (Nr.48) when in the Prussian service.

Otherwise the reasons for this complex reorganization are unclear. The Landgraf was certainly consciously attempting to remodel his army at least outwardly on Prussian lines, and ostensibly the new two-battalion organization was also intended to induce the French to believe that the strength of the Hessian infantry had doubled (in reality it may also have been calculated as a way of increasing the British subsidy). Ferdinand of Brunswick responded to the changes by commenting in July 1761 that 'I always count the Hessian infantry regiments as two battalions, despite their weakness and the fact that they do the job of [only] one battalion. I do this in order not to upset calculations made on this basis since the beginning of the campaign' – i.e. since before he realized that the additional battalions he had been promised did not actually represent an increase in the strength of the Hessian contingent.

All regiments had dark blue coats with various facing colours. In *c.*1748 Morier had depicted a very distinctive combination of dark blue breeches and buff or straw-coloured waistcoats, and this combination may have survived until the reforms of 1760 brought a much closer conformity to Prussian styles. At that time, if not before, both waistcoats and breeches were variously described as yellow, straw-coloured or white, which suggests that exact colours may have varied from issue to issue. Grenadier caps were Prussian in style, with tin or brass fronts according to button colour, as were the fusilier caps issued to two regiments in 1760.

Regimental distinctions, 1757 (with 1760 changes)

Garde or *Leibgarde zu Fuss* Red facings, white lace; tin grenadier cap plate with yellow 'bag'; red pompons with white centre

Capellan (1760, *Füsilier-Regiment von Berthold* – see Plate F2) Orange facings; brass cap plate, orange bag; red pompons with orange centre

Fürstenberg (1760, *Füsilier-Regiment von Gilsa*) Red facings (1760, black); brass cap plate, cream bag; blue pompons

Prinz Ysenburg Pale buff facings; brass cap plate, pale buff bag; white pompons

Leib-Regiment (1760, *Wutginau*) Red facings with no lapels; brass cap plate, red bag; yellow pompons

Grenadier-Regiment (1760, *2. Garde*) Ponceau-red facings; tin cap plate, red bag (1760, yellow); red pompons with white centre

Erbprinz (1760, *4. Garde/Leib-Regiment*) Yellow facings (1760, rose-red); tin cap plate, yellow (1760, red) bag; red pompons with yellow centre (1760, rose-red)

Mansbach White facings; brass cap plate, white bag; white pompons

Prinz Karl Blue lapels (1760, red); brass cap, red bag (1760, blue); white pompon with blue centre (1760, all blue)

This Knötel illustration depicts the uniform worn in 1785 by the Hessian 1. Bataillon Garde raised in 1760, the only new feature being the fur grenadier cap that had by now replaced the original tin-fronted mitre.

Uniforms of the pre-1760 Hesse-Kassel Leib-Garde zu Fuss/Regiment Garde, as reconstructed by Knötel:
LEFT **Grenadier. Dark blue coat and breeches, red facings, white lace, straw/buff waistcoat – see Plate F1 for details.**

RIGHT **Officer. Hat with rich silver lacing, white-over-red plume, black cockade. Dark blue coat with red collar, cuffs and lining, richly decorated with silver brandenburgs. Yellowish-buff smallclothes; silver-and-red sash; note gorget – silver ground, gold-wreathed blue cartouche – and spontoon.**

ABOVE **Grenadier of the Hesse-Kassel Infanterie-Regiment Graf von Hessenstein, 1749, as depicted in Knötel's *Uniformen-kunde*; by the outbreak of the Seven Years' War the *Inhaber* had changed and this had become the Regiment von Kanitz. Knötel shows the coat-facings, waistcoat, and the bag and pompon of the tin-plated grenadier cap as a buff/orange shade.**

Kanitz Buff/pale orange facings (later yellow – probably due to problems fixing former colour dye); tin cap plate, buff/yellow bag; buff/yellow pompon
Prinz von Anhalt Red facings; tin cap plate, red bag (1760, blue); white pompon with blue centre
Hanau Red facings; tin cap plate, dark rose-red bag; rose-red pompon with white centre

HESSIAN MILITIA

Like a number of other German states, Hesse-Kassel also boasted a Landmiliz or militia. These were ordinarily employed as garrison troops and to maintain order in the absence of a police force; however, the French invasion of Hesse saw them forced to take the field in 1758. The experience was not a happy one, although they performed rather better than might be expected of militia. On 23 July 1758, Prince Ysenburg was forced to make a stand at Sandershausen against the invading French army under the Duc de Broglie. Although badly outnumbered he had a strong position, and deployed his regulars on each flank with the three Militia units in the centre, supported by a scratch battalion of 'invalids'. For some time he held his own, but as the Militia took casualties they began closing in to the centre, gradually losing contact with the regular units on either flank. As those regulars in turn came under increasing pressure the Militia were soon all bunched together in the centre and firing on anyone who came near them, friend or foe. At this point Ysenburg rightly decided that enough was enough and ordered a retreat, which – surprisingly – was carried out more or less successfully.

Only dire necessity had prompted the employment of the Militia in battle, and the experiment was not repeated. Instead, in 1760 the three Militia regiments were reorganized into Garrison battalions of four companies each, and one standing battalion of Garrison Grenadiers with four companies. The uniforms worn by the Garrison battalions were presumably the same they had worn as Militia: plain-finished dark blue coats with red turnbacks and Swedish cuffs, straw-coloured waistcoat and breeches, and white-laced hats.

LEFT **Hessian Fusiliers, c.1760, by Fritz Kredel. The officer – note right shoulder cord – and NCO wear the orange facings and lining and gold lace of Regiment von Berthold (see Plate F2). The bookish-looking gentleman with the cane is a *Feldscher* or company clerk, all in plain dark blue lined with red. Far right, carrying a sheaf of straw, is an officer's servant dressed in an all-grey uniform, showing green at the turnbacks and in small button-loops on his waistcoat.**

Regimental distinctions

Wurmb Orange cuffs; tin or pewter grenadier cap plates, blue bags; white pompons with red centre

Gundlach White cuffs; tin cap plates, red bags; white pompons

Freywald Yellow cuffs; tin cap plates, yellow bags; yellow pompons

Prior to 1760 the grenadier companies had worn the uniforms of their parent units as above, but when the consolidated grenadier battalion was turned into a standing unit it adopted red cuffs, and caps with dark blue bags.

PRUSSIAN INFANTRY

At the very outset of the war the Rhine fortress of Wesel was garrisoned by six infantry battalions belonging to Fusilier-Regiments Nr.44 (Jungkenn), Nr.45 (von Dossow) and Nr.48 (Hessen-Cassel [sic]). It was hoped that the garrison commander, Gen de la Motte, might be able to hold out for some weeks in order to delay any French invasion and so give the Allies time to concentrate, but in the event that concentration was so much delayed that he had to evacuate the fortress and retire on Lippestadt.

This caused some awkwardness; since Gen de la Motte was merely the fortress commander, as soon as the garrison marched out of the gates the senior infantry officer, LtGen the *Erbprinz* of Hesse-Kassel (the man who was to embark on the complete reorganization of his army, described above, on succeeding as *Landgraf* in 1760) insisted on taking command of the force. He was manifestly incompetent to do so, but although Gen de la Motte complained to King Frederick the monarch declined to intervene; there was a danger that if the Erbprinz was displaced it could create difficulties with the Hessian contingent then serving under the Duke of Cumberland. Frederick appealed to Gen de la Motte to have patience: 'for Heaven's sake do me a favour and do not worry about rank. You know quite well that precedence is all he thinks about … so if you want to do me a really good turn, flatter him and be obsequious'. After some minor skirmishing, 'Old Fritz'

Hessian Line infantry uniforms, by Knötel:

LEFT *Fahnen-junker* of Infanterie-Regiment Prinz Karl. Hat with gold lace and red-on-white pompons. Dark blue coat with red collar, cuffs, lapels and turnbacks; gold lace edging on cuffs, cuff-flaps, lapels. White waistcoat and breeches. Dark blue regimental colour with lighter blue central cartouche bearing red-and-silver lion, below crowned red scroll with gold lettering; silver wreaths and grenades, gold cyphers.

CENTRE **Grenadier, Infanterie-Regiment Prinz Ysenberg.** Brass cap-plate, straw-coloured rear bag piped in white, straw-coloured pompon. Dark blue coat, straw-coloured facings and turnbacks, white lace button-loops on front and cuff flaps, brass buttons. Straw-coloured waistcoat and breeches, red neck-stock, white belts.

RIGHT **Musketeer, Infanterie-Regiment von Mansbach.** White lace and red pompons on hat; usual red neck stock. Dark blue coat and lapels, white cuffs, turnbacks and button-loops. Dark blue waistcoat and breeches; white belts.

withdrew the entire brigade before the Erbprinz could do anything damaging, but in the event Gen de la Motte's pessimism was justified: only some 900 men ever got back to Magdeburg, the rest having deserted en route.

All three regiments had collarless coats with red cuffs and turnbacks, but only Fusilier-Regiment Nr.48 had red lapels. Waistcoats and breeches were straw-coloured for Nr.44 and Nr.48 and white for Nr.45; all three units had black gaiters, and brass-fronted fusilier caps. The caps had a black rear 'bag' and headband (Nr.44), straw-colour and red (Nr.45), and all-blue (Nr.48). Other than these, and the lapels worn by Nr.48, the only real distinguishing features were the lace loops on the coats; Nr.44 had red with white tassels, Nr.45 white loops and tassels, and Nr.48 yellow loops with red tassels. Leather equipment for all three comprised broad whitened-buff belts with a black cartridge box slung behind the right hip, and the usual cowhide knapsack slung on the left together with a tin canteen and canvas bread bag.

Prussian fusiliers, as depicted in Knötel's *Uniformenkunde*. This is Regiment Nr.35, with straw-coloured collar, cuffs and smallclothes; see text for distinctions of Nrs. 44, 45 and 48, which served in the Allied garrison of Wesel.

TECHNICAL TROOPS

Like that of the cavalry, the performance of the Allied artillery was at first less than effective. Early practice seems to have been largely a matter of establishing batteries, assigning a suitable infantry escort, and then leaving them to their own devices. Factoring in a general shortage of guns – and those neither particularly modern nor mobile – it is easy to see why Ferdinand and his mentor Frederick were less than satisfied with the artillery arm.

The army's original artillery commander, the Graf von Schaumberg-Lippe, had a fair reputation as an artillerist, but his expertise lay largely in the science of gunnery rather than in the tactical use of artillery on the battlefield. While the strength of the artillery arm soon increased, in part by making extensive use of captured French guns, its tactical handling still lagged behind. This was exemplified by an unedifying dispute between the Graf von Schaumberg-Lippe and Gen Wangenheim at Minden over the question of deciding priorities for artillery fire, which so distracted all concerned that Ferdinand himself had to personally attend to the deployment of much of the Allied artillery. Consequently, when Schaumberg-Lippe received an attractive offer to enter the Portuguese service in 1762 Ferdinand parted from him with few obvious regrets.

Brunswick

To all intents and purposes the Brunswick artillery was a subordinate arm of the infantry, as its three companies had no heavy guns and were solely employed in manning the 'regimental' artillery. They wore plain dark blue coats with red cuffs and turnbacks, being distinguished from

HANOVERIAN INFANTRY

1: Grenadier, *Fussgarde-Regiment*, 1757
2: Musketeer, *Infanterie-Regt Hardenberg*, 1759
3: Musketeer, *Infanterie-Regt Sachsen-Gotha*, 1759

A

HANOVERIAN CAVALRY
1: Grenadier, *Grenadieren zu Pferde*
2: Cuirassier, *Kürassiere-Regt von Hodenburg*
3: Prussian dragoon, *Dragoner-Regt Nr.9 (Holstein-Gottorp)*

B

LIGHT CAVALRY
1: Prussian hussar, *Husaren-Regt Nr.5 (Reusch)*
2: Hanoverian hussar, *Luckner'scher Frei-Husaren*, 1757
3: Carabinier, Buckeburg contingent, 1758

C

HANOVERIAN LIGHT TROOPS
1: Mounted Jäger, *Freytag'scher Freikorps*
2: Grenadier, *Scheither'scher Freikorps*
3: Musketeer, 1st Battalion, *Légion Britannique*

BRITISH CONTINGENT AT MINDEN, 1759
1: Private, 51st (Brudenell's) Regt of Foot
2: Grenadier, 25th (Edinburgh) Regt of Foot
3: Trooper, 6th (Inniskilling) Dragoons

E

HESSE-KASSEL CONTINGENT
1: Grenadier, *Leibgarde zu Fuss*, 1760
2: Fusilier, *Fusilier-Regt von Berthold*, 1760
3: Musketeer, *Frei-Regiment von Gerlach*

F

BRUNSWICK CONTINGENT
1: Hussar, *Husarenkorps*
2: Officer, *Infanterie-Regt von Imhoff*
3: Dragoon, *Dragoner-Regt von Bibow*

TECHNICAL TROOPS
1: Hanoverian pontoneer
2: Hesse-Kassel artilleryman
3: Artilleryman, *Scheither'scher Freikorps*

H

the infantry by wearing straw-coloured waistcoats and breeches. Officers and NCOs had gold-laced hats, while ordinary gunners had yellow lace.

Drivers had essentially the same uniform, but with blue cuffs and grey turnbacks.

Britain

The basic administrative unit of the artillery was the company. Tactically, British guns were grouped in 'brigades' of light and heavy artillery, but unlike their German counterparts there is no evidence for the use of 'battalion guns' by British infantry units serving with the Allied army.

All Royal Artillery personnel wore dark blue coats with red facings, and yellow or gold lace according to rank. Officers were primarily distinguished from the rank and file by wearing red waistcoats and breeches, while the ordinary gunners and NCOs had blue smallclothes. For full dress, officers' coats and waistcoats were generously laced in the usual fashion, but on active service plain 'frocks' and unlaced waistcoats were the norm. Similarly, although white gaiters were supposed to be worn in full dress, for other duties officers had boots and all other ranks wore black gaiters.

At this date there was no corps of drivers as such, and civilian contractors were normally employed instead. Morier's group painting of artillery personnel at Roermond in 1748 includes a figure in a steel-grey coat with red cuffs and white lace, who appears to be a driver; but in 1756 the *Ipswich Journal* noted that 'The drivers attached to the train of artillery wear white frocks [smocks?] with the letters GR in red on their backs'. Given the lack of a military corps of drivers, it is striking that the performance of the Royal Artillery in Germany was distinguished by mobility; they not only came into action more rapidly than their German counterparts at Minden and Warburg, but proved capable of efficient tactical redeployment during battle.

Buckeburg

The Schaumberg-Lippe/Buckeburg contingent was – reasonably – organized on the presumption that as it would only ever take the field as part of a coalition force, and it was felt that it could do so more effectively by specializing in artillery than by attempting to field a more balanced 'army in miniature'. At the outset the contingent comprised a single battalion of infantry, theoretically numbering 820 officers and men, and supported by a single company of artillery with two light 3-pounder guns. By 1759 the artillery had acquired eight heavy 12-pounder cannon; and in the summer of 1761 there were 16 pieces in total, including siege howitzers. It is not clear where the gunners to man these additional guns came from. Some sources suggest that they were found by drafting men from the Carabiniers, but it seems rather more likely that they came from the infantry battalion; like the Sachsen-Gotha regiment, this was solely employed as an escort for the artillery train rather than as a line unit.

The infantry uniform was a blue coat with red collar, cuffs and turnbacks, and a white waistcoat

Print after Knötel illustration of the crew of an artillery piece of the Seven Years' War. Visible from left to right are the ramrod/sponge man, the gunner with portfire, the loader with satchel, the gunlayer, and a mounted officer section-commander.

and breeches. Musketeers had the usual black hat with white lace, and red-over-white pompons; the grenadier company was distinguished by blue cuffs, and a brass-fronted fusilier cap with dark blue bag in the Prussian style. The artillery had light blue or steel-grey coats and breeches, with black cuffs and red turnbacks, white waistcoats, and unlaced hats.

Hanover
At the outset of the war the Hanoverian artillery comprised six companies each of 67 officers and men, but under Ferdinand it was reorganized into four field brigades each of two to three companies.

All artillerymen wore light blue-grey coats, sometimes referred to as steel-grey, with red cuffs, lapels and turnbacks. Officers had straw-coloured waistcoats and breeches, while all other ranks had red waistcoats and straw-coloured breeches. Lace was yellow or gold according to rank, and equipment was buff leather. As with the infantry, they started the war with a generous amount of lace trimming on the lapels and waistcoats, but this was soon abandoned. Drivers had red coats with red turnbacks, but bright blue cuffs and lapels, with brass buttons in pairs. Waistcoats were straw-coloured, and buff breeches were worn with heavy boots; the hats were plain black.

Hesse
The original establishment of two companies was increased to three in 1757, with a total of 15 officers, 27 NCOs and 385 men including drivers, and in 1760 to five companies. These companies were only responsible for the heavy artillery, however, and by the end of the war there were four other companies providing personnel for the two light cannon assigned to each infantry battalion. The basic uniform for both officers and men was a dark blue coat with red facings, and a dark blue waistcoat and breeches. Drivers had loose white jackets, and round hats with red bands.

LIGHT TROOPS

The seemingly exponential growth in what were termed 'light troops' during the war was largely attributable not to any revolution in tactics, but to two closely related factors.

At the outset it was naturally recognized that reconnaissance and outpost work was best undertaken by light cavalry such as hussars and carabiniers, or light dragoons, in order to avoid dispersing and wearing out battle cavalry on such time-consuming duties.

With that in mind, a certain Rittmeister Nikolaus Luckner and his Free Company of Hussars were induced to exchange the Dutch service for the Hanoverian just prior to the commencement of hostilities. As the French were obviously engaged in exactly the same tasks, it was soon found necessary by both sides to back up these scouts by attaching infantry or Jäger companies to the light horse; and so the business of what became known as *Kleinkrieg* rapidly escalated, as this recruitment assumed a momentum of its own.

There was little that the Allies could do to expand their regular forces during the course of the war, other than – as already mentioned – by rather hopefully increasing the official establishment of existing battalions, and turning consolidated grenadier battalions into permanent units. This was partly because all the available native Brunswick, Hanoverian and Hessian recruits were needed to maintain the existing units, and partly due to the perceived practical difficulty of training new battalions up to pre-war standards. Instead the necessary increase in the size of the army was achieved by the creation of 'free corps' – independent or unattached units, supposedly recruited from neutral states such as Hamburg or Denmark, but all too frequently made up of deserters, former prisoners of war and other mercenary riff-raff.[2]

Frederick the Great himself was famously disdainful of such troops. As a rule these new corps lacked the discipline, training and equipment of regular units, and were employed almost exclusively in 'small war' operations or on garrison duties, simply because they were unfit to stand in a proper battle-line. There is no doubt that some of them acquired a certain expertise in this kind of work, but the net effect of pumping more and more men into this particular role was that the enemy were obliged to counter their efforts by doing likewise, so the numbers on both sides inevitably spiralled upwards to no great effect.

Conversely, the 'free corps' often had great difficulty in maintaining the necessary numbers in their ranks. Partly this was because their being so frequently engaged in skirmishing with the enemy led to higher casualties, and partly because the easier discipline and opportunities for plunder were counterbalanced by a lack of basic logistic support; allied to the drudgery of ceaseless outpost work, this all produced high rates of sickness and desertion.

Notwithstanding the tendency to fill out the ranks with ever more dubious (and occasionally exotic) material, a certain amount of reorganization and consolidation took place as the war went on. In late 1761 Ferdinand was compelled to raise an entire brigade of Chasseurs or

Knötel illustration of a Brunswick officer of the Husarenkorps (see Plate G1). Brown fur *Kolpack* with yellow bag, silver-and-red cords. Yellow dolman and breeches, blue cuffs and pelisse, silver cords and lace, black fur trim on pelisse. Horse furniture and sabretache blue with silver lace.

---

2 The promiscuous use of both German and French languages in 18th-century military contexts produced several different spellings, e.g. *Frei-Corps*; to avoid confusion, we use the style *Freikorps* throughout this text.

Jägers under Lord Cavendish, comprising four battalions of 'volunteers' drawn from the regular units in each of the four national contingents.

Brunswick

As one of the smaller Allied contingents, Brunswick contributed proportionately few light troops.

The **Brunswick Hussars** (see Plate G1) were raised late in 1759 with the aid of the inevitable British subsidies, and at first consisted of four companies each of 114 men plus a staff of 17, for a total of 473 men under Maj Anton von Roth. For the 1761 campaign the regiment was augmented to six companies totalling about 747 men, led by Maj Friedrich Adolf Riedesel zu Eisenbach (who was later to achieve some fame commanding the Brunswick contingent in North America).

A **Jäger corps** commanded by Col von Hoym was raised in 1759, comprising two companies of mounted Jäger zu Pferde and three companies or 'brigades' of Jäger zu Fuss, each notionally 95 strong but usually numbering rather fewer. Only the second company was equipped with rifles, the rest having to make do with ordinary muskets. In 1762 an additional company of each type was added, to give a notional total of 746 officers and men, including 13 gunners serving two *amusettes* – very light artillery pieces. As was customary, all the Jägers wore green coats; the mounted companies were distinguished by straw-coloured collars and turnbacks, while the foot companies had red. All wore green waistcoats and straw-coloured breeches, with black boots or gaiters, and the usual plain black hats with green pompons. All equipment was of black leather.

For most of the war these units comprised the totality of the Brunswick light troops, but in 1762 a **Light Infantry** battalion was raised as the Brunswick contribution to Cavendish's Jäger brigade (see above). Details of its uniform appear to be unrecorded; but the Light Infantry Battalion von Barner which served a decade later in North America had dark blue coats with black collar and cuffs and red turnbacks, white smallclothes, hats trimmed with white lace and black/white pompons, so a similar uniform may possibly have been worn in 1762.

In the same year a rather exotic unit entitled the ***Volontaires auxiliares de Bronswick*** was also formed, under Col von Rauch; its curious title reflects the fact that French was then the common 'lingua franca' in Europe, so from sheer necessity served as the 'official' language used within such units This one comprised three rather large companies of cavalry, totalling 338 officers and men, and three equally large companies of infantry mustering a further 417 all ranks. In common with many 'free corps' its composition was cosmopolitan in the extreme, and a substantial proportion of these Volunteer Auxiliaries appear in fact to have been Balkan deserters and prisoners trafficked by the Prussian army. At any rate, the cavalry comprised a company each of Husaren, Grenadieren zu Pferde, and Bosniaken, while the infantry were officially designated as grenadiers but were more commonly referred to as 'Turcos'. At the armistice they were handed back to the Prussians, who promptly

Knötel's reconstruction of Brunswick troops in Canada in 1776 is not irrelevant to the earlier period. The figure at left depicts the new Prussian-style uniform adopted by the old Karabiniere-Regiment von Bibow on reverting to dragoon status in 1772, but the uniforms worn by the others are unchanged since the Seven Years' War. Note the Jäger (right) in green coat and waistcoat, red facings and lining, and straw-coloured breeches; and (right background) a light infantryman in a blue coat with black collar and cuffs but no lapels, red turnbacks and white smallclothes.

disbanded them and dispersed the personnel into regular units.

Unsurprisingly, their uniforms are poorly recorded. The Hussars apparently had a dark blue uniform with yellow facings and cords, and black fur on the pelisse; a black *Kolpack* with yellow bag; and dark blue horse furniture edged in yellow. They thus seem to have been fairly conventional in appearance, but the Bosniaks were much more exotic. They supposedly had a bright blue jacket and Turkish trousers, with a dark grey kaftan trimmed with white, and a white fur turban wrapped around a red cap; they may also have been equipped with lances. References to grenadiers are slightly complicated by uncertainty as to whether they apply to the Horse Grenadier squadron, the infantry, or both. At any rate, they seem to have had blue coats (with a suggestion that the cavalry wore dark blue and the infantry light blue), with green facings, green waistcoats, and straw-coloured breeches with black boots or gaiters. Headgear is described as a *Kaskett*, which would suggest a cylindrical Balkan-style cap as worn by Pandours.

Britain

Britain contributed a surprising number of light troops, exclusive of locally raised units in British pay. The best known were the 15th Light Dragoons of Emsdorf fame; but the 87th and 88th Highlanders were employed as light troops from the outset, and in 1761 a third battalion known as Fraser's Chasseurs (or Jägers) was raised from volunteers out of the Line regiments. (Arguably, if counter-intuitively, the two British grenadier battalions should also be considered under the heading of 'light troops', since they were brigaded with the 87th and 88th Highlanders and almost exclusively employed on Kleinkrieg operations.)

The **15th Light Dragoons** had: 'A short coat lapelled and turned up with dark green, white lining and white waistcoat, with a green collar, broad white buttons and buttonholes, two white shoulder straps, two pairs of white linen breeches, jockey boots and spurs, the cloak with a green cape and lined with white. Instead of a hat, a copper cap enamelled with black, brass crest with white and red hair, the front turned up, with the King's cypher and crown painted or enamelled on it, a flap rolled up behind in order to cover the neck on occasion. A tanned leather cartouch-box instead of a pouch, with a running spring swivel, and a tanned leather sword belt'. A contemporary painting by David Morier largely confirms this description, though the 'flap' on the helmet actually took the form of a green turban with two ends hanging down at the rear; he also shows a red cockade on the left side of the helmet, as well as a lion-mask at the front of the brass 'crest' or comb.

The **Highlanders** were formed around a nucleus of recruits originally intended for the Black Watch, but instead formed into first one and then two battalions and shipped to Germany rather than North America. Although separately numbered, throughout their existence they served in effect as two battalions of the same corps, with officers frequently being

Von Natzmer's Uhlans were a light horse unit on the Prussian payroll. Curiously, Knötel's reconstruction of their Turkish-style light blue and white uniform appears to be very similar to that described for the Bosniak company of the 'Volontaires Auxiliaires de Bronswick' raised in 1762, although the latter are said to have had red caps and grey kaftans instead of the light blue and white shown here.

Scottish Highland soldier as depicted in Maj George Grant's *New Highland Military Discipline* of 1757, which was published shortly before the raising of the 87th and 88th Highlanders for service in Germany.

cross-posted between the two units, and so far as can be ascertained both wore the same uniform. From portrait evidence, this comprised the usual Highland dress of flat blue bonnets, short red jackets with medium green facings, plaids or kilts in the familiar Army tartan, and red and white chequered stockings. Officers' portraits show pale buff-coloured waistcoats but, as noted elsewhere, this was a common affectation, and it is likely that the rank-and-file had red. Officers had gold lace, edging the collar and cuffs and in alternate bastion and round loops at the front of the jacket. All equipment was of black leather, comprising a sword belt over the right shoulder supporting a basket-hilted broadsword on the left hip, and another holding a belly-box in front.

There is no indication of any distinguishing features that may have been worn by **Fraser's Chasseurs/Jägers**, although precedent suggests that at the very least they probably stripped the lace from their various regimental coats.

Britain also maintained a substantial auxiliary unit in the five-battalion *Légion Britannique*. As its title suggests, this was a somewhat cosmopolitan crew, largely comprised of Germans but including Swiss and Dutch (and at least one Russian). While it is usually considered a part of the Hanoverian Army, it was paid for by Britain and ultimately had a British commanding officer, MajGen John Beckwith. Each Legion battalion primarily comprised four musketeer companies notionally of about 125 men, for a total battalion establishment of 500 all ranks, although it is unlikely that any of the battalions actually succeeded in parading anything like this number. In addition to the four musketeer companies each battalion also had an organic cavalry element in the form of a 100-strong dragoon company. In practice, however, all of the Legion's dragoon companies were normally consolidated as a single unit; eventually this was regularized, by the creation in 1762 of a distinct cavalry regiment under Rittmeister von Hattorf.

All five battalions of the Legion had straw-coloured breeches, but otherwise their uniforms were completely different. The 1st Battalion (see Plate D3) had light blue coats with straw-coloured cuffs and turnbacks, and straw-coloured waistcoats; the 2nd Bn were in medium blue with scarlet facings and white waistcoats; the 3rd Bn had orange facings and waistcoats; and the 4th and 5th Bns wore red coats, the former with bright blue facings and straw-coloured waistcoats, the latter with black cuffs, white turnbacks and white waistcoats. The 1st Battalion had brass buttons (and gold lace for the officers' hats), while the others had tin. The hats worn by the rank-and-file were unlaced and decorated only with green cockades (and probably green leaves as well, when they could be had). Equipment was of buff leather with black cartridge boxes. The dragoon companies wore the same uniforms as their parent battalions, and had red horse furniture, trimmed in yellow for the 1st Bn and white for the others. There appears to be no evidence that they received a new uniform on being consolidated into a regiment under Capt von Hattorf.

Buckeburg

In addition to the artillery train and its attendant infantry escort, the contingent also included a small unit of carabiniers – light cavalry armed with short hussar-style carbines – and a supporting company of Jägers. The former (see Plate C3) were issued a black *Kollet* with red facings and straw-coloured breeches, with black armour and fur-trimmed helmets. The accompanying Jägers had dark green coats with yellow collar and cuffs and green turnbacks, yellow waistcoats, green breeches, plain black hats, and the usual boots.

Hanover

The Hanoverian light troops fell into two ill-defined categories: those which were specifically raised as part of the Hanoverian Army, and those paid for by the British government.

It would appear that there were no light troops of any description prior to the war, but in May 1757 a Jäger corps was formed by Graf von Schulenburg; as was customary, this comprised two companies, one of mounted and one of foot Jägers. At about the same time Luckner and 54 of his 'free hussars' came over from the Dutch service (see above), and from this modest beginning a considerable expansion soon took place.

Luckner's Hussars mustered 90 men by the end of 1757, but in the following year they doubled their strength to two companies totalling 8 officers and 174 men. In 1759 they redoubled to four companies, and by 1760 there were no fewer than eight companies, paired in four squadrons, with an official establishment of 32 officers and 632 hussars. The original uniform of Luckner's light horse is depicted as Plate C2. However, as the combination of black *Flügelmütze* 'winged cap', green dolman and pelisse, and red breeches was virtually indistinguishable from the uniform of the French Army's Chasseurs de Fischer, a different outfit was soon adopted – probably during the first increase in establishment. This comprised a white dolman and breeches, and a red pelisse with yellow cords and black fur edging; the 'winged cap' was replaced with a grey fur *Kolpack* with a red bag, and the original green barrel-sash was exchanged for a yellow one, though the original yellow boots were retained. The saddle cloth was red with yellow trimming, and officers seem to have had a dark brown fur shabraque with red vandyked edging.

The expansion of the **Jäger corps** was at first less dramatic, with only two additional foot companies being added in the course of 1758, and then an additional mounted company during the following year. At that point Col Freytag succeeded to the command of the corps, and the strength was raised considerably thereafter. It was expanded to no fewer than six companies each of Jäger zu Pferde and Jäger zu Fuss, and while the establishment of the mounted companies remained at 106 all ranks, that of the infantry companies went up from 156 to 206 – on paper, at least. In the long run this expansion proved unsustainable; in 1762 Freytag's Jäger corps was amalgamated with another raised by Maj von Stockhausen, to make a single battalion of just four companies, with a total of 804 officers and men. Stockhausen had first raised a Schützen battalion in 1759, comprising one grenadier and two Jäger companies; although he added two companies of Jäger zu Pferde the following year it seems unlikely

Troopers of the Scheither'scher Frei-Karabiniere (left) and Luckner'scher Frei-Husaren in Hanoverian service, c.1760, as depicted in Knötel's *Uniformenkunde*. As was not uncommon, the white uniform with green facings and waistcoat worn by the cavalry element of Scheither's Freikorps was totally different from that worn by his green-coated infantry. The hussar of Luckner's corps is illustrated wearing the later uniform – white dolman and breeches, red pelisse and *Kolpack* bag, yellow lace and boots – adopted after it became clear that the original (see Plate C2) was dangerously similar to that of the Chasseurs de Fischer in the French army.

that the full 500-man establishment was ever achieved, hence the amalgamation with Freytag's unit in 1762.

The uniform of both corps was broadly similar (see Plate D1 for a Jäger zu Pferde of Freytag's). All wore the traditional dark green coats, with green facings, green waistcoats, tin buttons, straw-coloured breeches, plain black hats, and either boots or gaiters depending on whether they were mounted or on foot. Horse furniture for the mounted element of both corps was green with white or silver trimming. The only distinguishing features were the absence of lapels from the coats worn by the mounted element of Stockhausen's corps, and the curious grenadier caps worn by some of his men. These resembled the *Kaskett* then being worn by some Prussian and Austrian light troops, with a cylindrical leather skull and low frontal plate, similar in size to fusilier caps but more rounded. In the case of Stockhausen's grenadiers the caps were green and bore the arms of Hanover on the front in silver; although it is uncertain whether these were embroidered, or if the front was tin with a green-painted ground, the latter seems more likely. In theory, as Jägers all of the men in both corps should have been armed with rifles, but it is more likely that ordinary infantry muskets predominated, and these were certainly carried by Stockhausen's grenadiers.

Scheither's Freikorps was formed by Capt H.A. Scheither in May 1758 as part of the process of expansion of light troops following the lessons of Ferdinand's first campaign. Initially it comprised a single company apiece of carabiniers, grenadiers and Jägers, but by 1761 it had increased somewhat to muster four companies of carabiniers and two of fur-capped grenadiers, besides the Jäger company and an artillery detachment. There are also suggestions that there may have been a troop of Uhlans, but this was most likely the one which ended up in the Brunswick Auxiliary Volunteers as 'Bosniaks'.

The carabiniers had a very pale straw-coloured coat or *Kollet* with dark green collar, cuffs, turnbacks and trimming, a straw-coloured waistcoat and breeches, and green horse furniture trimmed in white. Hats were plain black with a green cockade; as their designation suggests, they were armed with straight swords and short hussar-style carbines slung on a swivel belt. Both the musket-armed grenadiers and rifle-armed Jägers wore green coats with green facings, and straw-coloured waistcoats and breeches; apart from the grenadiers' brown fur caps (see Plate D2) they were further distinguished from Freytag's men by a vandyked lace pattern on collar and cuffs.

To improve their self-sufficiency each infantry company had a six-strong detachment of *Zimmermen* or carpenters, wearing the same uniform but distinguished by a low-crowned helmet with a crest and a green turban trimmed with white, bearing the white horse of Hanover on the front. The corps' artillery were probably detached from the regulars, as they appear to have worn the same steel grey/blue uniform with minor distinctions as to the cuffs and waistcoat (see Plate H3).

Hesse-Kassel

The Hessian contribution was surprisingly small in relation to the overall size of the contingent. It comprised a regiment of hussars and the predictable Jäger corps, and later a 'free regiment' was contributed to Cavendish's multi-national Chasseur/Jäger brigade.

Possible reconstruction of an infantryman of Trumbach's Freikorps (Volontaires de Prusse) in that corps' final uniform, c.1762. White hat-lace, red pompons; black neck stock. Dark blue coat; red collar, lapels, cuffs and turnbacks; white metal buttons. White smallclothes and belts, black gaiters. (Painting by Bryan Fosten, 1992)

The **Husaren-Korps** had actually been raised in 1744 as a single squadron of two companies, and served with the Hessian contingent in Scotland during the last Jacobite Rising. At the outbreak of war in 1756 it was expanded into a small regiment by adding a second squadron, and the reorganization of 1760 saw these doubled to four squadrons by the simple expedient of redesignating each company as a squadron – without making much effort to increase the actual number of sabres, except on paper. They wore a light blue (or 'Attila-blue') dolman and pelisse with red collar and cuffs and yellow cords, and buff breeches. The *Kolpack* was of brown fur with a red bag and yellow cords. One source cites white fur trim on the pelisse, but it may also have been brown. Sabretache and horse furniture were both light blue trimmed in yellow.

The Hessian **Jägers** could also boast a respectable pedigree, tracing their history back to the beginnings of the Hessian army during the Thirty Years' War. By 1757 there were two companies of Jäger zu Fuss, and by August 1759 two companies of Jäger zu Pferde had been added. Interestingly, they appear to have been unaffected by the 1760 reorganization, although from that time there was a tendency to refer to the foot companies as a 'battalion'. The uniform comprised the traditional green coat, with red collar, cuffs and lapels, and green smallclothes.

The light infantry unit raised for Cavendish's light brigade in 1762 was initially designated the Chasseur Battalion von Rall, before becoming the **Frei-Regiment von Gerlach.** When it was first formed the men would no doubt have worn the uniforms of their parent units, but later adopted the blue uniform with green waistcoat and breeches illustrated as Plate F3.

Prussia

Prussian light troops serving with the Allied army comprised in the main five squadrons of regular hussars, three drawn from Regiment Nr.5 (Reusch) and the other two from Nr.7 (Malachowski). There were additionally four hussar squadrons belonging to a regiment known as the Freikorps or Frei-Husaren Bauer, raised by Ferdinand in 1760 (see commentary to Plate H1) and taken into Prussian pay the following year. Ferdinand also raised an infantry unit, the Freikorps von Trümbach – also known as the *Volontaires de Prusse* – which was taken onto the Prussian payroll as Frei-Bataillon Nr.11.

A trooper of Husaren-Regiment Nr.5 (Reusch), otherwise known as the Black Hussars, is illustrated as our Plate C1. The Yellow Hussars, Nr.7 (Malachowski), had a broadly similar uniform except for the colour of the dolman and *Scharawaden* leggings, and the decoration with white lace and cords. Their pelisse, however, was blue with black fur; in the Prussian service this garment was rarely worn slung except for parade, but was worn buttoned as an additional jacket in cold weather. Bauer's Free Hussars had a black *Flügelmütze* trimmed with yellow, an all-dark blue uniform with yellow collar, cuffs, lace and cords, black fur trim on the pelisse, and a red-and-yellow barrel-sash.

The **Freikorps von Trümbach**/*Volontaires de Prusse* was raised in 1759 with one dragoon, one Jäger and four infantry companies. By 1760 the cavalry element was two squadrons of hussars, which later passed to

Reconstruction of a dragoon of Trumbach's Freikorps, 1759. Black hat cockade and green pompons. Green coat and waistcoat; red collar, shoulder strap, cuffs and turnbacks; brass buttons. Straw-coloured breeches under buttoned green *Scharawaden* leggings; white belts. Horse furniture green, edging yellow with two red stripes. (Painting by Bryan Fosten, 1992)

NEXT PAGE **Knötel's** reconstruction of a mounted Jäger, foot Jäger and grenadier of Freytag's Jägerkorps (see Plate D1); coats and waistcoats are plain green, breeches straw-coloured for the Jäger zu Pferde and white for the infantrymen. Note that the latter are erroneously depicted wearing boots; a contemporary illustration clearly shows the usual thigh-length gaiters.

Freytag's Jägerkorps – see caption page 41.

PLATE COMMENTARIES

A: HANOVERIAN INFANTRY

Superficially there was a strong resemblance between the uniforms worn by King George II's Hanoverian and British troops. In both services the infantry wore red coats, and regiments were distinguished by contrasting facing colours on the cuffs, lapels and turnbacks. The Hanoverians also wore cloth grenadier caps rather than the brass- or tin-fronted ones favoured by the other North German armies. There were, however, a number of differences and variations in style. In about 1748 the Swiss artist David Morier depicted lace trimming on the edges of cuffs, lapels and waistcoats, just as in the British Army; but the later *Gmundner Prachtwerk* shows the lace restricted to button-loops only, perhaps as a wartime economy measure. More strikingly, where most British units had red waistcoats and breeches, their Hanoverian counterparts had facing-coloured waistcoats and straw-coloured breeches; indeed, the experience of serving alongside the Hanoverians may have been a significant factor in British units switching from red to straw or white breeches in the 1760s.

A1: Grenadier, *Fussgarde-Regiment*, 1757

The Fussgarde were distinguished by the dark blue facings unique to this regiment. The musketeer companies of the two battalions served under Spörcken at Minden, taking part in the advance against the French centre, but the two consolidated grenadier companies were permanently assigned to headquarters security duties throughout the war. Gauntlets are depicted by Morier, who indicates that they were worn by all Hanoverian grenadiers, but they were probably restricted to guard mountings. Perhaps the oddest feature of the Hanoverian uniforms, but one that is clearly depicted in all of the *Gmundner Prachtwerk* illustrations, is the large bunch of oakleaves attached to the headdress – odd, because this was traditionally the Imperial/Austrian field-sign.

the Freikorps Bauer. The original dragoons reportedly wore green coats with red collar, Swedish cuffs and turnbacks, yellow buttons, and green *Scharawaden* with high boots. The hussars seem to have had a brown fur *Kolpack* with white bag, white dolman faced with yellow, blue pelisse with white fur and lace trim, blue-and-white barrel-sash and blue overalls. The Jägers had a light green coat with red Swedish cuffs and turnbacks, white buttons, a green waistcoat, and straw-coloured breeches. By *c.*1760 the infantry companies wore a dark blue coat with light blue collar, Swedish cuffs and lapels, red turnbacks, white buttons, and the light blue smallclothes common among Free Corps units. It is possible that by 1762 the facings had finally changed to red and the smallclothes to white, with red pompons on white-laced hats (see illustration, page 40).

A2: Musketeer, *Infanterie-Regiment Hardenberg*, 1759

This *Musketier* also displays some typical features of Hanoverian uniform, including the pompons or cord-pulls in the two side corners of the hat, in this case coloured red and orange. Hardenberg was one of the better Hanoverian regiments; at Hastenbeck it was part of the outflanking force under Breidenbach and Dachenhausen which recaptured the key Obensburg position towards the end of the battle, thus causing near-panic amongst the French – leading to the unusual spectacle of both armies hastily withdrawing from the battlefield at the same time. At Minden it took part in Spörcken's advance, and when Scheele's brigade, to which it belonged, was effectively crowded out, it determinedly kept up with the Fussgarde and participated in the destruction of the French cavalry.

A3: Musketeer, *Infanterie-Regiment Sachsen-Gotha*, 1759

This regiment was a mercenary contingent hired by the Hanoverian government in 1756. Dressed at first in white coats with green facings, it changed to red coats on being taken into the Hanoverian Army proper on 25 January 1759. There is a suspicion that it was not regarded as a particularly efficient unit; it had seen little action prior to that date, and was then permanently assigned as an escort to the artillery and bridging train. Apparently its most notable exploit was to contrive to deploy well back from the fighting at Minden, in a position that effectively blocked the advance of the Allied cavalry, thus materially contributing to the unfortunate chain of misunderstandings that followed.

B: HANOVERIAN CAVALRY

B1: Grenadier, *Grenadieren zu Pferde*

The Horse Grenadiers were in effect the dragoon element of the Guard cavalry, and by all accounts were well mounted but rather old-fashioned in their training, which emphasized precision in movements at the expense of speed, and the use of firearms rather than cold steel. While they were present at most of the major engagements, including Hastenbeck and Minden, their war record was rather uneventful, and in 1762 they were amalgamated with the Garde du Corps. Both units wore red coats, but while the latter had dark blue facings the Grenadieren zu Pferde had black cuffs and lapels. These were originally edged with gold lace, but this was later dispensed with as an economy measure. The unit did, however, retain the elaborately embroidered grenadier cap featuring the arms of Hanover, as well as other infantry/grenadier accoutrements such as cartridge boxes and match cases on their belts.

B2: Cuirassier, *Kürassiere-Regiment von Hodenburg*

Rather more effective were the heavy cavalry, represented here by a trooper of the Hodenburg regiment. While still officially designated as cuirassiers, none of the Hanoverian heavy cavalry actually wore armour by this period, other than metal 'secretes' or openwork metal skullcaps under their hats. Dragoon regiments were very similarly dressed, and were largely distinguished from the Kürassiere only by having facing-coloured lapels and right shoulder aiguillettes. When mounted they wore the customary jacked leather knee-boots, but when off duty – as here – they normally changed into more comfortable shoes (at one point Ferdinand had to order their shoes to be turned over to his barefoot infantry). Incidentally, observers tended to be struck by how slovenly the troopers' stockings and breeches looked when they were not wearing their boots.

This particular regiment was the oldest in the army, having been raised as far back as 1645, and was also known as the Cell'shes Reiterregiment. For a time it had a reputation as an unlucky unit, with no fewer than three of its Inhabers being killed in action during the War of the Austrian Succession, and a fourth, von Schlutter, killed in the opening days of the Seven Years' War. His successor, von Hodenburg, gave the lie to this by commanding it for the duration – most notably at Hastenbeck, where two squadrons took part in the wildly successful attack on the French right flank.

B3: Prussian dragoon, *Dragoner-Regiment Nr.9 (Holstein-Gottorp)*

Serving alongside the Hanoverian cavalry was an excellent brigade of Prussian dragoons in cornflower-blue coats, represented by this trooper of the brigade commander's own unit, which had coat-colour facings. Holstein-Gottorp's distant origins as a mounted infantry regiment are marked by the wearing of an aiguillette or shoulder knot, as was common to most dragoons of the period. (This feature is sometimes hopefully if rather unconvincingly interpreted as a survival of the old 'arming point' used to fasten armour on to the 'arming doublet' worn beneath, but it is far more plausibly explained as recalling the skein of slow-match once carried looped over the shoulder by both dragoons and infantry corporals.)

Hanoverian Fussgarde, as depicted in Knötel's *Uniformenkunde* (see Plate A1). This illustration seems intended to depict the battle of Minden, but while the musketeers of the Fussgarde certainly participated in Gen von Spörcken's advance, the grenadier companies did not. Note in the background the regimental colour with the arms of King George II, as carried by all Hanoverian infantry units.

C: LIGHT CAVALRY

C1: Prussian hussar, *Husaren-Regiment Nr.5 (Reusch)*

In addition to the two regiments of dragoons, the Duke of Holstein-Gottorp's Prussian cavalry brigade included three squadrons of these 'Black Hussars' and two from Regiment Nr.7 (Malachowski), the 'Yellow Hussars'. Easily the more recognizable was Regiment Nr.5, with its black uniform topped off with a decidedly piratical *Totenkopf* badge on the *Flügelmütze* hussar cap. British officers had served alongside Hanoverian and other German troops before, but nevertheless close acquaintanceship with the various hussar units that made up such an indispensable part of the Allied forces sometimes seems to have come as a something of a culture-shock. The Black Hussars attracted particular notice, and one rather bemused officer wrote of them to a correspondent as 'a nasty looking set of rascals, the picture you have in the shops in London is very like them though it does not represent their rags and dirt – they make no use of tents; at night or when they rest they run their heads into some straw or any stubble and the rest of their persons lies soaking in the rain. It's said that some private hussars have this campaign got about 2,000 German crowns, nay some advance it to pounds. They drink more brandy than water and eat I believe more tobacco than bread'. Notwithstanding this first impression, less than 50 years later aristocratic British cavalry officers would develop an obsession with replicating some aspects of their appearance – but while expressing great enthusiasm for daring raids in the Zeithen tradition, they proved lamentably uninterested in the outpost work that was supposedly the primary role of hussars.

C2: Hanoverian hussar, *Luckner'scher Frei-Husaren, 1757*

While Luckner's Free Hussars proved themselves a workmanlike crew, very adept at scouting and skirmishing, they were also undoubtedly more interested in picking up any plunder that came their way, and from time to time – as

at Warburg – their behaviour induced near-apoplexy among senior officers. This was certainly not helped by their commander's reputation as a poor disciplinarian, and his casual attitude to military accountancy. Johann Nickolaus Luckner was the son of an innkeeper from the Upper Palatinate. Entering the Bavarian Army in 1737, by 1745 he was an Oberleutnant in the Ferrari Hussars, from where he transferred to the Dutch service. In 1757 the then-Rittmeister Luckner entered the Hanoverian service with 54 of his men; as usual, they gave themselves out to be genuine Hungarians, but the close resemblance of their original uniform – shown here – to that worn by the Chasseurs de Fischer in the French service suggests that the 'Dutch' unit was largely formed of former members of that corps (which may also explain their rivalry). Luckner was nevertheless a spirited and successful partisan leader who rose in rank each year, to lieutenant-colonel in 1758, colonel in 1759, major-general in January 1760 (adding the aristocratic 'von' to his name), and lieutenant-general in 1761. After the war he accepted a corresponding appointment in the French army, but was guillotined during the Revolution.

The need to be more easily recognizable in skirmishes with Fischer's men, and equally to avoid being shot up by their own side, soon prompted the unit to adopt a different uniform, comprising white dolman and breeches and a red pelisse, topped off by a grey fur *Kolpack*, although they retained their cherished yellow boots.

C3: Carabinier, Buckeburg contingent, 1758

One of the most outlandish-looking units to serve in the Allied army were the Buckeburg Karabiniere, raised by Graf Wilhelm von Schaumberg-Lippe and commanded by his equerry, Maj Johann Casimer von Monkewitz. With a nominal strength of only 75 men, their tactical effectiveness was

The *Uniformenkunde* illustration of the Prussian Husaren-Regiment No.5 (von Reusch) – the Black Hussars (see Plate C1), who displayed a death's-head badge on their 'winged cap'.

obviously limited and, unlike Luckner's unit, the company only ever appears to have been used for scouting and outpost duties. The only serious fight they were involved in was apparently the defence of the vital Rhine bridgehead at Rees on 5 August 1758. This reconstruction is tentatively based on Richard Knötel's interpretation of a painting dating from about 1765, when the unit was no longer in existence. Evidently intended to recreate the appearance of the infamous Schwarz Reiter of old, the troopers not only rode all-black Spanish stallions, but wore a black-dyed elk-skin *Kollet* and, initially, near-complete sets of 17th-century cuirassier armour lacking only the thigh-pieces. Officers, by contrast, wore highly polished 'white' armour in equally antique taste, with large infantry-style gorgets. While unquestionably dramatic, this ensemble was soon found impractical for a light cavalry unit, and in 1759 all but the cuirass and helmet were discarded. The helmet was embellished not only with the fur turban depicted here, but with a narrow green band running underneath it bearing the inscription *Pulchrum Mori Succurrit in Extremis* ('In danger, a beautiful death lies waiting') – a sentiment that was doubtless a great comfort to the men who wore it…

D: HANOVERIAN LIGHT TROOPS

D1: Mounted Jäger, *Freytag'scher Freikorps*

Freytag's Jägers were the first unit of light troops raised for the Hanoverian Army, and as usual comprised both mounted and dismounted companies. The original commanding officer, Graf von Schulenberg, appears to have been an unenterprising sort; it was under his successor Freytag that the unit made its name, although he never quite matched his rival Luckner's reputation, and seems to have been regarded as more reliable than brilliant. As was customary for Jäger units the uniform was green, and topped with a plain black hat. The mounted companies had boots and buff leather breeches as shown, while the foot companies had straw-coloured breeches and grey or brown gaiters.

D2: Grenadier, *Scheither'scher Freikorps*

Scheither's Freikorps was raised in May 1758 and originally comprised just three companies, but soon expanded dramatically; by 1761 there were four companies of mounted carabiniers, two companies of grenadiers and one of Jägers, totalling about 900 officers and men. Most unusually for the Allied army, the grenadiers wore fur caps; secondary sources sometimes refer to these as being Austrian in style, but they were most likely captured French headgear. (This was certainly not an unknown practice; for example, the entire British 5th Foot adopted the caps that they captured from the Grenadiers de France at Wilhelmsthal in 1761.) The Jägers of this corps wore a similar uniform with unlaced black hats, but the Karabiniere had pale straw-coloured coats similar to those worn by many cuirassier regiments – which rather reinforces the impression that, initially at least, Scheither clothed his men by scrounging whatever he could find lying around in depots and stores.

D3: Musketeer, 1st Battalion, *Légion Britannique*

The Légion Britannique was clothed in a distinctly *ad hoc* fashion in keeping with the very mixed nature of its human material. Each of its five constituent battalions was dressed in a completely different uniform, and the 1st was recorded as having this bright blue coat with straw-coloured facings and smallclothes.

The missions assigned to the Legion were many and varied. In July 1760, all five battalions were detached, along with the Hessian Hussars and a battalion of Jägers, to capture the bridges over the Diemel at Liebnau and Trendelburg. At Warburg, the Legion mounted spirited demonstrations against the French front to cover the outflanking march of the main army; afterwards it was ordered to join in the pursuit of the defeated French, but the abandoned baggage trains proved too much of a temptation, and they joined Luckner's men in plundering the town. Most of the Legion were discharged at Munster on 2 January 1763. This was anticipated with some trepidation, but in the event a surprised Gen Conway reported that it was 'executed without the least Tumult or Disorder, which considering how this Corps is composed chiefly of deserters of all Nations… was more than was expected, [especially] as several [of their] demands remain unsatisfied'. This docility, he believed, was because they were about to be enlisted into the Prussian service; but in fact only enough men volunteered to make up one battalion – which was perhaps just as well, since their commanding officer, MajGen Beckwith, had been planning to use them in a coup aimed at seizing the city of Munster for Prussia.

E: BRITISH CONTINGENT AT MINDEN, 1759

E1: Private, 51st (Brudenell's) Regiment of Foot

The basis of this figure is a near-contemporary painting by Edward Penny of a sick British infantryman, presumably serving in Germany, being given money by the Marquis of Granby. The unidentified soldier's regiment is tentatively identified here as the 51st Foot, by the gosling-green facings. The only other units serving in Germany with similar facings were the 5th and the 24th Foot, but in both cases the Swiss artist David Morier had earlier painted both in quite different uniforms. The green breeches are most unusual for an infantryman, but Penny seems to have been conscientious in depicting uniforms; while there are no other known illustrations of the 51st at this time, this may well have been a regimental affectation by a newly raised corps. Also worthy of note are the stiffened tops to the black gaiters.

Notwithstanding their having only been raised as recently as 1755 the 51st were in fact the first British troops to arrive in Germany, landing to serve as a garrison for Emden in early April 1758. At Minden they were brigaded with the 20th and 25th Foot under Col William Kingsley, marching in the second line of Spörcken's division as it embarked on its famous advance against the French centre. The 'Minden Roses', which legend tells us were plucked by the division as they went into action to serve as an impromptu field sign, actually came from a hedge further down the battlefield where they halted to reorganize *after* the French had been utterly defeated.

E2: Grenadier, 25th (Edinburgh) Regiment of Foot

However, Minden roses were not picked at all by the grenadier companies of the six British infantry regiments present, since they were assembled into a consolidated grenadier battalion under Col William Maxwell, and this served in Wangenheim's division over on the Allied left. This grenadier of the 25th (Edinburgh) Regiment is based on one of David Morier's paintings. Although most British

LEFT **The original uniform of the Luckner'scher Frei-Husaren (see Plate C2): green dolman and pelisse with yellow lace, and red breeches. The close resemblance to that worn by the Chasseurs de Fischer, who were performing the same duties on the same front for the French army, accounts for their switch to a more distinctive uniform.**

RIGHT **The French Chasseurs de Fischer, c.1745, as depicted in Knötel's** *Uniformenkunde***, with red pelisse and breeches and green dolman with yellow lace. The resemblance between this unit and Luckner's Free Hussars was even greater in the early part of the Seven Years' War, by which time Fischer's unit had changed to a green pelisse.**

infantrymen had by this time discarded the cheap swords or 'hangers' still theoretically worn as a secondary weapon, grenadiers retained them as a mark of their elite status. No regulation pattern was prescribed, but as a general rule curved blades and basket hilts were popular.

E3: Trooper, 6th (Inniskilling) Dragoons

Famously, the British cavalry played no part in the Allied victory as a result of Lord George Sackville's refusal to obey orders to advance; conscious of their failure (actually arising from imprecise and conflicting orders), they supposedly sang not a single note of the celebratory *Te Deum* after the battle. Our rather disgruntled-looking trooper of the 6th (Inniskilling) Dragoons wears an entirely typical uniform, with facing-coloured waistcoat and breeches. His status as a dragoon is marked by his cartridge box, musket and bayonet. Although conventionally referred to as a carbine, the external dimensions of this weapon were identical to those of the later Short Land Pattern firelock, with a 42in barrel and the same 0.75in bore as the ordinary infantry musket.

F: HESSE-KASSEL CONTINGENT

F1: Grenadier, *Leibgarde zu Fuss*, 1760

The Leibgarde zu Fuss could trace its unbroken lineage back to the Regiment von Geyso that fought at Lützen in 1632. After the Thirty Years' War it first became the Kassel Palace Company, and then, when the Landgraf Karl formed his standing army in 1684, the Leibgarde zu Fuss. Notwithstanding this pedigree, in the complex 1760 reforms the regiment was redesignated as 3. Garde, being superceded in first place of seniority by a ceremonial Garde-Bataillon.

Gerry Embleton's reconstructions of the cut of typical British infantry regimental coats, from Morier and other contemporary and near-contemporary primary sources (see Plate E). The half-lapels could be buttoned across for extra protection when in the field, either entirely or only for half their depth.

This grenadier provides a good example of the metal-fronted mitre caps favoured by most such units from northern Germany. In this case the front plate was of tin, embossed with the Langraf's cypher and the lion of Hesse. The infill of red paint, seen here as depicted by Knötel, is tenative, but it may have been applied when the caps were first issued and then subsequently polished away. The regiment's musketeers had the usual cocked hats, distinguished by white scalloped lace and red-over-white pompons. Also of interest here are the distinctive dark blue breeches, depicted by the Swiss artist David Morier in his series of paintings executed for the Duke of Cumberland in c.1748. Originally they were worn by all Hessian infantry, making it easy to distinguish them from the similarly dressed Brunswick troops, but there is some uncertainty as to when they were abandoned in favour of the more conventional straw- or yellow-coloured garments being worn by 1761. It is possible that this change may have occurred as early as 1750, but it is more likely that it was part of the effort to make the army more Prussian in appearance in 1760.

F2: Fusilier, *Fusilier-Regiment von Berthold*, 1760

As part of the 1760 reforms two infantry regiments, Von Gilsa and Von Berthold, were redesignated as Fusiliers. The change in status was purely cosmetic, and other than the probable adoption of white or straw-coloured breeches in place of blue the only real alteration in appearance was the replacement of the cocked hat with the distinctive brass-fronted cap depicted here. Copied from the Prussian style, this cap as worn by the Fusilier-Regiment von Berthold had a dark blue 'bag' rather than orange as previously worn

by the regiment's grenadiers; the caps worn by the fusiliers of Fusilier-Regiment von Gilsa followed their grenadiers by having bags in the facing colour of creamy yellow. Originally raised in 1683, the then Infanterie-Regiment von Capellan had seen action at Hastenbeck in July 1757; on 5 August 1758 at Mehr the regiment was part of Imhoff's force which repulsed the French attempt on the Allied bridgehead at Rees, and it also fought at Lutterberg on 10 October. The following year it was involved in the debacle at Bergen, when Ferdinand of Brunswick rushed, and botched, an attempt to retake Kassel; it had better luck later in the year at Minden, when it was part of Von Wutginau's brigade, and it went on to fight in 1760 at Emsdorf and Warburg.

F3: Musketeer, *Frei-Regiment von Gerlach*

By contrast, very little is known of the Frei-Regiment von Gerlach, reconstructed here from a painting by Richard Knötel. Other than the obligatory Jäger corps and squadron of hussars Hesse raised very few light troops, in part because the 1760 reorganization meant that nearly all the available recruits had to be pushed into the ranks of the regular army – notwithstanding the detrimental effects on efficiency – rather than segregated in auxiliary units such as this. Nevertheless, in 1762 Ferdinand required each of the national contingents to supply a Jäger or Chasseur battalion for a light brigade being formed under Lord Cavendish, and this was the Hessian contribution, originally known as the Chasseur Battalion von Rall. Once again, as in the Prussian Army, their second-class status was indicated by the wearing of coloured waistcoats and breeches, in this case green, rather than the white or straw-coloured breeches sported by regular units.

G: BRUNSWICK CONTINGENT

G1: Hussar, *Husarenkorps*

Like the Hessians, the Brunswick troops served in His Britannic Majesty's Army not as an allied contingent, but under the terms of a subsidiary bilateral agreement with the British government. One of the terms of the Convention of Kloster-Zeven in 1757 was a repudiation of that agreement, and accordingly the Brunswick contingent were instructed by their ruler to return home. However, they were intercepted by the Hanoverian Gen von Zastrow when just on the point of crossing over to the French lines. With one exception the officers agreed to continue serving with the Allies – the appointment of Ferdinand of Brunswick to command the army was obviously a significant factor – and thereafter there were no doubts about the Brunswick contingent's loyalty.

As usual, the Brunswick Hussars were supposedly raised around a substantial nucleus of genuine Hungarians, all of them presumably deserters from the Austrian Imperialist forces. Their true nationalities are questionable; there is no doubt that like most Freikorps volunteers they were drawn from an ever-shifting polyglot population of adventurers, and differed from the mercenaries that roamed Germany during the Thirty Years' War only in probably being more regularly paid and properly uniformed – albeit in a deliberately anarchic style, quite unlike that of the overdressed hussars of a century later. In this case the yellow uniform may have been inspired by that worn by the two squadrons of Prussian Hussar Regiment Nr.7 serving with the Allied army, but is more likely to have been chosen simply to be as different as possible from the blues and greens generally favoured by French hussars.

G2: Officer, *Infanterie-Regiment von Imhoff*

By contrast, this smart-looking officer is virtually indistinguishable from his colleagues in the Prussian service. While his uniform is obviously made from better materials than those served out to the rank and file, and bears all the customary marks of rank such as metallic braid decoration and a sash loosely knotted around his waist, another indicator of his status is the tailoring. Coats worn by the rank and file followed Prussian fashion, being tightly cut and relatively short, with permanently turned-back skirts; but officers in all the German states – including Prussia – demonstrated that they were gentlemen by continuing to wear very full-cut frock coats. A relatively new regiment formed only in 1748, this unit had a good record; it fought at Hastenbeck, and under LtGen von Imhoff at Mehr in the hard battle to secure the Allied bridgehead over the Rhine at Rees. The regiment was also engaged at Bergen, Minden, Fulda, Ziegenhain, Vellinghausen and Wilhelmstal.

G3: Dragoon, *Dragoner-Regiment von Bibow*

The status of the regiment represented by this trooper is a little unclear. They did not form part of the original contingent hired by Britain, and do not appear in the Allied order of battle until 1759, by which time they were redesignated as Karabiniere and employed as heavy cavalry. However, at least one source states that prior to that date they were involved as dragoons in *Kleinkrieg* operations, perhaps against Imperialist rather than French troops. The colour of the waistcoat is uncertain, and one source states that it was green.

British infantry grenadier's mitre cap, here of the 49th Regiment of Foot but more or less typical of the designs used by all regiments (see Plate E2). The front and the headband at the bottom rear are in regimental facing-colour; the 'little flap' at the front, and the back of the cap, are red, and the binding of white tape. Unless a regiment had a particular traditional badge the front bore a crowned 'GR' cypher, and the 'little flap' always bore the white horse badge of the Hanoverian dynasty. (Reproduced by permission of the Trustees, National Army Museum, London)

H: TECHNICAL TROOPS

H1: Hanoverian pontoneer

The large number of rivers that cut across the area of operations in western Germany, including the Rhine and the Weser, obliged Ferdinand's army to become unusually adept at bridging. Civilian barges had to be hired in Holland for the Rhine crossing near Rees, but this arrangement obviously had its limitations, and in early 1760 three 'brigades' with light bridging equipment were raised under the command of Maj Bauer, Ferdinand's Quartermaster-General. At first each brigade included a company of hussars, but soon these were themselves assembled into a small regiment, the Frei-Husaren von Bauer, which was taken onto the Prussian establishment. The uniform of these bridging brigades is uncertain; that depicted here is recorded as being worn by pontoneers in the Hanoverian service, and it seems likely that the reference is to Bauer's corps.

H2: Hesse-Kassel artilleryman

Both gunners and officers of the Hessian artillery wore dark blue coats, waistcoats and breeches, with red collar, cuffs, and turnbacks, black hats with red pompons and white or silver lace according to rank, and black gaiters. Equipment was largely copied from Prussian models, with a broad whitened-buff belt supporting a large powderhorn and a drag-rope on the right hip, with loops on the front for prickers.

H3: Artilleryman, *Scheither'scher Freikorps*

Some of the larger 'free corps' units had their own organic artillery elements, and this gunner of Scheither's corps is based on a contemporary illustration in the Royal Collection at Windsor. The uniform depicted is very similar to that worn by regular Hanoverian artillerymen, but lacks the regulars' half–lapels on the coat; it features a steel-grey rather than a red waistcoat, and displays the distinctive lace pattern on collar and cuffs worn by all of Scheither's men.

INDEX

From the Caribbean to the Atlantic: a Bi

The Barbados Railway

Barbados Light Railway

Trains run daily to Bushy Park for Crane Hotel and the Bathsheba Coast.

Charming Scenery   **Bracing Breezes**   **Good Sea Fishing**

Same day return trips on Wednesdays and Sundays. For particulars of Train Service see Company's Time Table.

For Special Tourist Excursions, etc., apply to
G. V. de LA BASTIDE, C.E., Manager.

Jim Horsford

A Locomotives International Publication

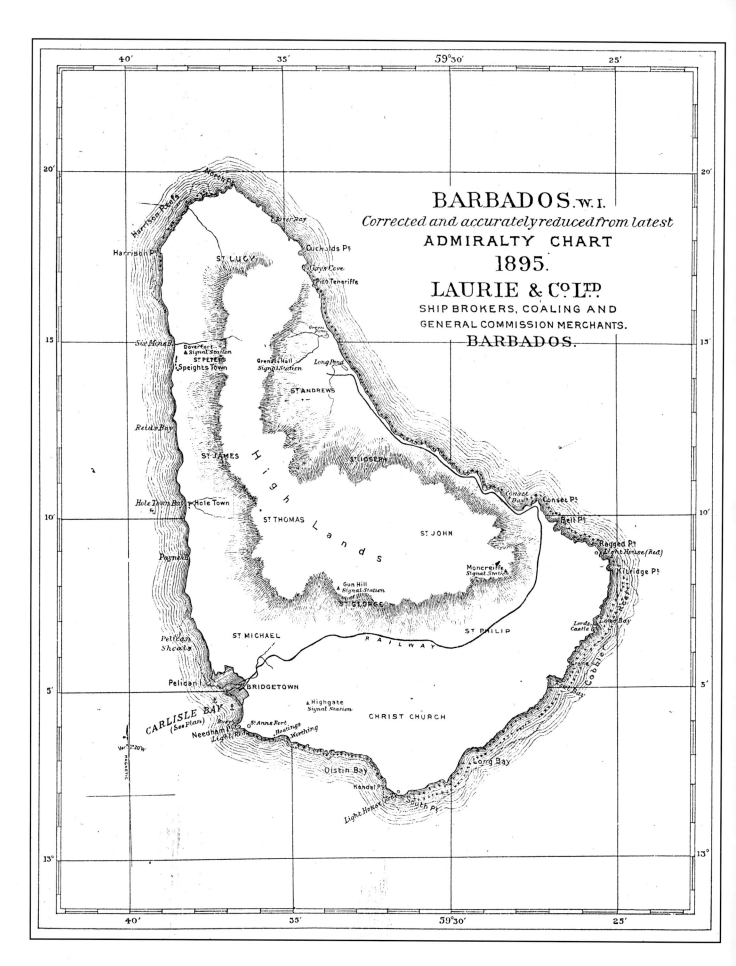

1895 Map of the island of Barbados

From the Caribbean to the Atlantic: a Brief History of
The Barbados Railway
Jim Horsford

Contents

Front Cover: This tinted lithograph from 'The Graphic' of 18th February 1882 shows the first train to arrive at Carrington's Point, hauled by one of the 2-4-0 locomotives built by the Avonside Engine Company, and inset is an impression of Bridgetown station.

Rear Cover: Two stamps were issued showing Barbados Railway scenes, the original photographs for which have been reproduced elsewhere in this book. The site of Bathsheba station is these days occupied by the Rail Road Cafe, whose presence is advertised with this colourful enamel sign, one of the few indications that there was once a railway there.

ISBN 1-900340-12-7. First published 2001. This edition © 2004 *Locomotives International* and Jim Horsford.
All rights reserved. No part of this book may be reproduced or transmitted in any form or by any means without prior written permission from the publisher.

Second edition. Published by Paul Catchpole Ltd., The Haven, Trevilley Lane, St. Teath, Cornwall, PL30 3JS, England
e-mail: editor@locomotivesinternational.co.uk Internet home page: www.locomotivesinternational.co.uk

Edited and typeset by Paul Catchpole, printed and bound by County & Pinewood, Broadheath, Altrincham, UK.
British Library Cataloguing in Publication Data. A catalogue record for this book is available from the British Library.

Introduction

Some old photographs in my late Father's albums alerted me to the existence of a railway on Barbados. As a young English boy, in 1950s' northern England, my Father's family seemed very exotic, from a place far distant from England called "The West Indies". On their visits to England, they proved to be very different folk to the average reserved post-war English person, and to me, since we never went there, the West Indian connection was very tenuous.

In the 1980s, after my Father's sudden death, all this changed. His photograph albums, of which we'd never spoken, came to me, and I finally realised that there had been a small railway on Barbados. When I finally got to visit the island, and to meet large numbers of my family there, I also discovered more about this railway.

Over time, I collected old picture postcards of the line, did some research in the Barbados Museum and elsewhere, and gradually built up quite a dossier on the railway. It turned out that the Barbados Railway had a chequered career, and it is my pleasure to retell its story here. This book is dedicated to all the Horsford clan who have descended from Trinidadians Frank and Agnes Horsford, but, in particular, this is written in memory of my late Father, David Russell Horsford.

One of the photographs which started off this whole exercise - a snapshot in my late Father's photograph album of a group ladies at Bathsheba station in the early 1920s. They have been identified as Miss Louie Toppin, Miss Bree Parkinson and Miss Stanley (Nanan) Toppin.

Photographic records

Obtaining sufficient and appropriate photographs of the railway has proved most difficult. All those included in this book have come into the Author's possession, and have been included in the book regardless of condition, quality etc. Photographs taken in the 1880s have survived - more or less intact - despite the ravages of time. Inevitably, they have suffered from being in a hot, tropical climate with (for many years) perhaps inadequate storage conditions. They are included, for their subject matter, not their quality. Other more recent, and perhaps useful photographs, have eluded inclusion, as suitable copies have simply not been located. An example of this is a series of photographs published in Barbados in newspapers and magazines some thirty years or so ago - often with interesting subject matter - but simply no longer traceable. To obtain suitable, publishable copies has proved not to be possible.

Several archives have successfully been traced, and these are acknowledged below:

DJH   photographs and postcards from the Author's collection.
DRH   photographs from the album of my late Father,
         David Russell Horsford.
FJH   photograph from the album of my late uncle,
         Frank Horsford.
DB   photographs from the father of David Badley,
         whose family also spent times in Bathsheba.
BNT   photographs from the collection of the Barbados
         National Trust.
BMHS   photographs from the collection of the Barbados
         Museum & Historical Society.
PS   Documents from the archives of Peter Simpson.
MK   photographs courtesy of Mary Kerr.

Acknowledgements

Many people have helped enormously during the preparation of this book. In particular, I would like to mention the following:

The late Dorothy de C. Boyce (my aunt), who identified many of the family's photographs, and whose memories of the Barbados Railway are reproduced in this book.

Betty Carrillo Shannon and Maris Corbin of the Barbados Museum & Historical Society, for their help in locating some of the Museum's photograph collection.

Paul Foster of the Barbados National Trust, for arranging copies of much of the Barbados National Trust's collection of railway photographs.

Mary Kerr, postcard expert and general historian, Barbados. Her stalwart support in the preparation of this book is particularly

acknowledged.

Norman Hudson, postcard expert and friend, who guided this book from inception to publication.

Peter Simpson, whose extensive archive remains of Law & Connell records have proved most helpful in the book's preparation

All the detailed maps of the railway were drawn by the Author.

There are several contemporary comments and expressions in this book which could cause offence today. The Author apologises if their inclusion (which is for the sake of completeness only) does cause offence, and wishes to be dissociated entirely from such comments.

A History of the Barbados Railway

"The old time people used to say that the Barbados Railway was
mentioned in the Bible, among the creeping things of this Earth".

Introduction

Barbados is a small Caribbean island, only 21 miles long and 14 miles wide. It is the most easterly of the islands of the West Indies, being approximately 100 miles from its nearest neighbours, St.Lucia and St.Vincent, in the Windward Islands chain. Unlike its neighbouring islands, however, Barbados is generally low-lying, being composed of coral rather than having volcanic origins. Despite the relatively flat character of much of Barbados, the island reaches 1,100 feet above sea level in the north-east. This upland, hilly area is known as the "Scotland District".

Perhaps because of the island's relative flatness, Christopher Columbus did not sight Barbados on any of his four voyages to the West Indies from 1492 onwards. The Portuguese were the first Europeans to find the island. It is known that explorers from Portugal had anchored briefly off Barbados in 1536. In fact, it was the Portuguese who gave the island its name. They referred to it as "Los Barbados", meaning "the bearded ones", thought to be a reference to the island's Bearded Fig trees. There were no attempts to settle or colonise the island at that time. Much later, in 1625, a group of English adventurers landed on the west coast (near today's Holetown) and claimed the 166 square miles of Barbados for King James I. By this date there was no sign of the island's former Arawak or Carib indian inhabitants. The first English settlement of Barbados began two years later when, on 17 February 1627, eighty English settlers and ten black slaves landed on the island.

Sugar-cane was first brought to Barbados soon after, in 1637. Initially, it was used to produce rum. Thereafter, the success and development of the crop was striking and the island's plantation system was to become established as early as the 1650s. The growing of sugar-cane and the manufacture of sugar-products was

Barbados General Railway Company share certificate, 1845. (DJH)

A tinted postcard showing the railway at Bathsheba in the early 20th Century 2'6" gauge era. The train is headed by a Baldwin 2-8-2T whose conversion to oil firing is indicated by the squared-off bunker. (DJH)

BARBADOS LIGHT RAILWAY AT BATHSHEBA, BARBADOS, B. W. I.

to create great wealth for the small group of landowners and was to have a profound influence on both the island's economy and its population from then on. The majority of today's population is descended from the African slaves who were brought to Barbados to work the sugar plantations.

Even though the record years of sugar production in Barbados are now over - approximately 200,000 tons being produced in 1957 and 1967 - and although tourism is now the island's chief earner of foreign currency, thousands of Barbadians still depend on the island's sugar industry.

Unlike many of the Caribbean islands, which had been fought over by the European colonial powers and which had changed hands on several occasions during the seventeenth and eighteenth centuries, Barbados was to be administered as a British colony uninterruptedly from 1625 onwards. This unusual continuous rule by one colonial power ensured that Barbados was to enjoy a relatively high degree of stability and continuity in its government and administration. Three hundred years of colonial rule came to an end when, on 30 November 1966, Barbados became an independent state and a member of the Commonwealth of Nations. The island's population is currently about 265,000, of whom approximately 100,000 live in Bridgetown, the island's busy capital and chief seaport which grew out of a small quayside town of some 6,000 inhabitants.

"Railway Mania"

In the mid-nineteenth century, "railway mania" was sweeping the United Kingdom. It is not surprising that news of this transport revolution led to calls for the construction of railways in Britain's many overseas colonies. In the case of Barbados, it was felt that a railway would further develop the island and its infrastructure. Primarily, it would assist the all-important sugar-cane

industry by transporting its produce to the main port (Bridgetown) for export.

Unfortunately, the railway that was eventually to be built on Barbados was, from the outset, both an anachronism and a dubious financial enterprise. It got through two gauges and five different owners during its difficult existence, finally withering away in 1937. It appears to have been a railway that even the redoubtable Colonel Stephens (of UK light railway fame) would have balked at taking on. Indeed, some of Stephens' more obscure branch-lines in Britain were as main lines when compared to the one in Barbados.

Nevertheless, the Barbados railway had great character. Certainly, it created much enjoyment for the thousands of visitors to the island's Atlantic coast, particularly during the early decades of the 20th century, when tourism was beginning to take off in the West Indies.

Most of all, though, the Barbados railway had immense charm and character.

Bridgetown to Speightstown - "The Barbados General Railway"

The first railway promoted on the island was intended to run between its two principal settlements, namely Bridgetown and Speightstown (the latter then enjoying rather more prominence than it does today). The railway was proposed in 1845, at an early stage of Britain's railway mania, but failed to be realised when the promoters raised only a fraction of the line's construction costs. It was proposed to be of between 4ft 6in and 5ft 6in gauge, with numerous branch-lines to connect sugar factories to the main line. However, by 1850, only around 3% of the capital had been raised and the scheme was dropped.

The 3ft 6in-Gauge Era - Bridgetown to St. Andrew's

The next definite proposals for a railway emerged in 1873, proposing the construction of a railway from Bridgetown to St.Andrew's. This scheme also proceeded with difficulty. Eventually, an Amending Act of Parliament in 1878 succeeded the original 1873 Act. It is reported that the engineer, Robert Fairlie, renowned for his expertise in light and narrow-gauge railways, visited the island and played a decisive part in the proposals. In 1877, the Board of Directors revealed the following details of the line:-

It was to be of 3ft 6in gauge.
It was to have "American-style" passenger carriages (assumed to be carriages with single interior saloons with open balconies at each end?).
There were to be seven stations on the line, namely -
    Bridgetown
    Valley
    Carrington
    Bushy Park
    Codrington College
    Bathsheba
    Belleplaine

Paragraph 55 of the General Conditions of the Specification for the railway also gave instructions for the ordering of the following rolling stock:

Four Locomotives
Six composite 1st/2nd-class carriages
Five third-class carriages
Ten open goods wagons
Six covered goods wagons
20 sugar wagons

Whether this remained the full complement of the railway's initial rolling stock, as delivered, remains unknown at the time of publication. Similarly, no details of their manufacturer etc are available. However, the railway certainly acquired the four locomotives. From contemporary photographs, it is suggested that the above list had been somewhat enlarged by the time of the opening of the line.

Construction of the line

Construction commenced on Saturday, 23 June 1877. The ceremony is reported to have been held at a site about a quarter of a mile below Newcastle House. This location is some distance from the alignment as finally constructed and substantiates traditional stories that the route as constructed differed from the original proposal. A map dated 19 July 1880 detailed the "Abandoned portion of Previous Deposit shewn thus....". It clearly shows an alignment between Bushy Park and Bathsheba very different to the one finally constructed. In fact, it showed the line running very close to Codrington College and Newcastle House. This alignment is illustrated in the map opposite.

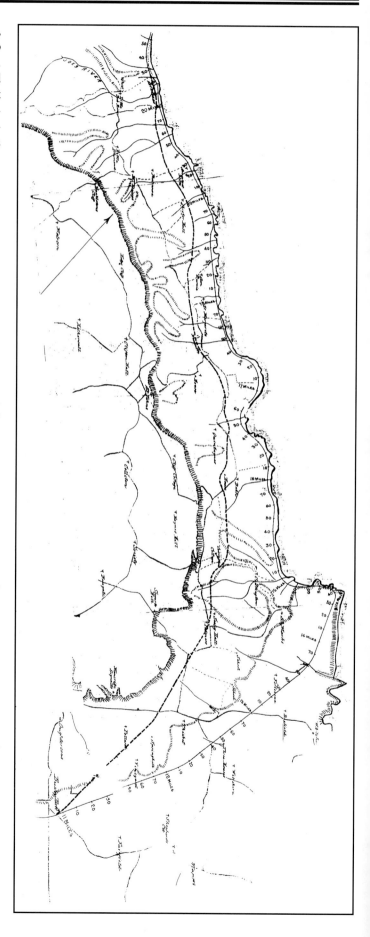

If the railway had been constructed on this original alignment, it would have averted more than one of the problems from which the completed route suffered thereafter. It is said that the alignment was changed at the instigation of the line's contractor who felt it more to his advantage to construct the line to the revised alignment.

Despite the animated scenes reported on that day in June 1877, construction of the line proceeded slowly. Legal and financial difficulties continued to persist, and so it was not until May 1879 that the contract for the construction of the line was finally signed.

1881 - The opening of the line

In early 1881, it was felt that construction was sufficiently advanced to warrant the engaging of a driver and a foreman from England to train the local labour force. The new railway's General Manager arrived too, a Mr Grundy from the Great Western Railway. Mr Grundy was unable to prove his capabilities as he died later the same year, reportedly from contracting yellow fever during construction works at the Constitution River in Bridgetown. His son succeeded him as General Manager.

By October 1881, it was felt that the line was ready for opening as far as Carrington. It was duly opened on Thursday, 20

October 1881. The Barbados Herald reported on 24 October that-

"Large numbers of persons from the town (were) availing themselves of the pleasure trip into the country and the novelty of this kind of locomotion in Barbados. We have observed a fair number of the labouring people amongst the passengers".

The train journey to Carrington took 40 minutes, and the service consisted of two return trips daily. The fares were -

Single (Bridgetown to Carrington):
First class   2/-
Second class   1/4d
Third class   6d

Return fares were charged at one and a half times the single fare, and were valid on the day of issue only.

The early days of operation

The first public concern over the quality of the construction of the line soon emerged. By 27 October, the local press announced "No Passenger Trains will run until further notice". The Globe assured its readers that, in any event, the opening on 20 October

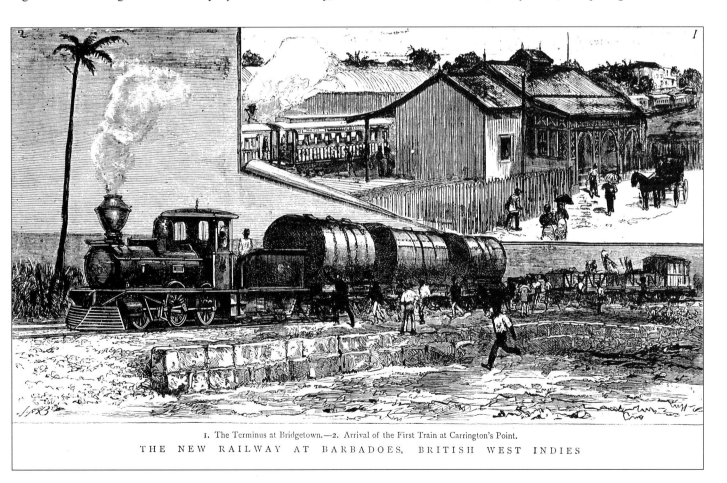

1. The Terminus at Bridgetown.—2. Arrival of the First Train at Carrington's Point.
THE NEW RAILWAY AT BARBADOES, BRITISH WEST INDIES

The first train arriving at Carrington, as depicted in 'The Graphic', 18 February 1882. (DJH)

An 1890s view of a Belleplaine-bound train crossing Long Pond Bridge. Already the piers of the bridge are causing concern, and the second one has been strengthened in a rudimentary manner, even at this early stage of its life. (DJH)

St. Andrew's Coast

J. R. H. Seifert & Co., Barbados.

had merely been "experimental" and that "arrangements were incomplete, the terminus being unfinished, the line being only tested". There were suggestions that the condition of the track had caused a carriage to derail on the first day. If so, this had possibly precipitated the closure.

After the line had reopened on 15 December, The Herald reported that "The line had been levelled and accommodation for passengers is all that could be desired". The obvious implication from this was that the track had not been level before. This was tacit acknowledgement that all had not been well in the construction of the line. In the line's subsequent history, worse was to come.

The Amending Act of 1878 had stipulated that the line was to be completed by 31 December 1882. It was not, and, in August 1882, a Bill was introduced to extend the completion date by a year, which was approved, albeit reluctantly by all reports.

The opening of the line through to Belleplaine (St. Andrew's) went unrecorded, but the Saturday, 18 August 1883 edition of The Herald printed an account of a journey over the whole line. The train arrived safely at Belleplaine and the dignitaries were able to "walk about and chat and wonder why the Railway should have ended so abruptly among barren sand hills?" This only-too-true observation was another early indication of the fragility of the railway.

The newspaper report also mentioned that the Chairman hoped that the Company would be able to extend the line to the public road past the Alms House, "provided that they could obtain the requisite power for borrowing more money". No doubt, this was a reply to the earlier references to the location of the line's terminus. The return to Bridgetown was also reported as being smoother than the party had been led to expect from local newspaper articles. Was this a further reference to the parlous state of the line?

From a civil engineering point of view, the line clearly was not built to a very high specification. The Rules, Regulations and Bye-Laws of 1883 gave the following instructions to railway staff:-

"22. BELLE GULLY BRIDGE

"Trains must travel over this bridge at reduced speed."

"23. CONSETTS AND LICORISHE INCLINES

"Great care must be exercised both up and down these inclines and both guards and drivers must have their trains well under control; guards must in all cases ride in the last vehicle, and every exertion must be made to stop runaway vehicles that may become detached from a train whilst it is ascending before the impetus has become too great".

Despite its inauspicious start, and uncertain construction and operation, the line's early years seem to have been quite successful. In 1890, it is reported that freight traffic reached an all-time high, but the dependency of the railway on the success of the sugar crop showed up the following year when freight receipts fell from £13,000 to £9,500.

Optimism for the future prevailed, and a scheme to fill-in the Constitution River was suggested. This would allow lighters to draw up alongside wharves adjacent to the railway's terminus, thereby avoiding the need for the quayside extension through Bridgetown's busy streets to the outer Careenage (the outer harbour). Despite the optimism, however, there was no depreciation fund being built up, and, when powers to borrow further funds were unsuccessful, the Company had to draw increasingly on its own financial resources for repairs.

This occurred to such an extent that, eventually, there were no funds even for routine maintenance and repairs.

By 1892, the Atlantic coast section of line was wearing badly. Numerous landslides, following heavy rainfall on difficult terrain, caused appreciable problems for the company. Its earlier civil engineering on this section was clearly developing faults. The

An early view of Bridgetown Station. The first, single-storey, station building nearly completed, with other structures being built alongside. In the platform are bolster wagons carrying rails, while the second track holds much of the railway's initial rolling stock. (BNT)

Bridgetown Station during construction, with one of the Avonside 2-4-0s in evidence. This photo was taken at a similar time to the one above. (BNT)

An early view of a freight train arriving in Bridgetown. The open wagons carry barrels - puncheons of molasses, while the vans contain sacks - of sugar? - all for transhipment at Bridgetown to deep-sea vessels. The loco is 2-4-0 no. 1. (BNT)

An early view of one of the Avonside locos and initial passenger rolling stock. The rear coach holds first and second class accommodation, the other is first class only. Preceding the 2-4-0 heading the train is the contractor's loco 'St. Michael' (BNT)

bridges and culverts developed problems and the viaduct over Long Pond, near the line's terminus, was reported by the Inspector to need "careful watching in the wet season" because of the tendency of the river to alter course (the report in 1934, which effectively decided the line's fate, was also scathing about the design and construction of Long Pond Bridge).

It appears, too, that the line had been constructed of different weights of rail, varying between 35lbs and 55lbs to the yard. The lighter rail was totally unsuitable and the company tried to replace it with 46½lb rail as quickly as it could. In 1893, the inspector reported that "the question of heavy renewals or the use of lighter rolling stock cannot be delayed much longer".

In the spring of 1894, Walter Merrivale became manager of the railway, and during this period the company introduced the "Penny Train". This was an attempt to increase patronage of the railway by the less affluent members of Barbadian society. It worked to some extent, and was reported to have carried lots of church outings and the like, but probably generated little additional and much-needed revenue. It did get a mention in the local press, however:-

"November 5, 1895 - From the Barbados Railway - On and after November 2, the first Penny Train will leave Town at 5.20 a.m. instead of 5.30; the second at 6.15 a.m. instead of 6.30; the third at 6.50 a.m. instead of 7.05 a.m. and the fourth at 7.30 instead of 7.45, returning from Three Houses at 8.33 instead of at 8.45 and arriving in Town at 9.53 instead of 9.28."

"The following is a list of the only crossings in addition to the regular Stations at which any train will then stop on the first section - Constitution Gate, Tweedside Gate, Kingston House, Licorish, Two Mile Post, Valley and Constant".

The notice was signed by W. Merrivale, Attorney and Managing Director.

The above suggests that several Penny Trains ran in the mornings for working people rather than for outings, stopping at several places in the Bridgetown suburbs before stopping also at several intermediate townships and estates along the route to Three Houses.

By 1896, things had deteriorated to a dire situation. A petition for voluntary winding-up was made to the Barbados Parliament. This was rejected. Instead, the company had to apply for additional borrowing powers for, amongst other things, the intention to finance an extension to Speightstown.

Across on the Atlantic coast section, matters had reached crisis point. The condition of the rails had "in many places lost over one half of the thickness of their flanges, in fact some are to a knife edge". Much of the rail on this exposed section had been in situ since opening in 1883, and, in the extreme climatic conditions - constant salt spray from the Atlantic and frequent heavy tropical rainstorms - were fast disintegrating. The storms in November and December 1896 were almost the last straw, and parts of this coastal section were totally destroyed and had to be completely rebuilt.

About this time, the Government Inspector, a Mr Law (of the firm of consulting engineers Law & Connell), reported that he could not describe the line as being in proper working order - despite an improvement since his last inspection! Rolling stock was "inadequate", and the locomotives and coaches were of too heavy a construction for the line, the whole of which needed re-ballasting in any case.

On 2 September 1897, Mr. J.Connell wrote a hand-written letter to Mr. L. Bert Esq. It read as follows:-

"The following is a report of the engines, rolling stock, workshop, tools, buildings etc of the Barbados Railway Company Ltd.

"I have carefully inspected the engines and such of the

Bridgetown Station after the September 10th 1898 storm, still 3'6" gauge. (DJH)

TRAIN LINE BARBER, BARBADOS.

NATIVE CHILDREN ON RAILWAY LINE, BARBADOS.

carriages, waggons, vans etc that were at the Bridgetown terminus, on the date of my inspection having found that there was little change in the condition of the rolling stock since a previous thorough inspection, I took part in during the early months of this year. I on the same day of my inspection sent out a competent man to take the numbers of the remaining waggons etc that were scattered about the Railway.

"Gauge.
The gauge of this Railway is 3'-6" and the rolling stock is fitted with a central spring buffer and lock coupling.

"Engines.
"Engine known as No.2 built by Avonside Engineering firm weight when loaded 20 tons four coupled tank (??) engine with leading bogie has a cracked tube plate, and when in use carries steam at a reduced pressure, the side and horn plates are very cut into, by the side action of the driving wheels, axle boxes bad. This engine has very little work left in her. The motion work is in fair order.

"No. 3 and 4 Vulcan Engines weighing when loaded 28 tons are six coupled tank engines with leading and trailing bogies outside. Cylinders 12 1/8th diameter and 17 inch stroke working at a pressure of 120 lbs per square inch. The side valves are worked by link motion driven by overhanging cranks. The boilers of these locomotives have been patched, and the fireboxes are beginning to show signs of wear. Leaks are to be seen at firebox

Bathsheba, Barbados, British West Indies.—25841.

stays; the motion work of these engines is in fair order.

"Axle boxes are very worn. Blast pipes are -----. These engines have still some work in them, and if new boilers and other small repairs were carried out, they would serve for a considerable time.

"No. 6, built by Hawthorn. A small 7½ ton locomtive with four coupled wheels, outside cylinders of 3/16th base(?) and 11 inch stroke, working at a pressure of 100 lbs to the sq. in has been recently overhauled. The boiler is the weak part of this engine. The motion work, frames etc is in fair order. Has still some service.

"Nos 6 and 7 have been already disposed of.

"Carriages

"These consist of 4 Groves pattern 1st class, 7 Groves pattern 3rd class, 2 double bogies 1st class and 3 double bogie 3rd - 2 passenger cars constructed on waggon frames, in all 17 passenger cars. These cars are built on the American principle and are entered by a door at each end.
"The iron frame wheels and axel (sic) boxes, stays, buffers and brakes of these coaches, although very rusty, are in fair working order. The woodwork on some carriages is beginning to rot, and the coverings of others are not weatherproof.

"Waggons.

"Sugar trucks, or waggons without sides. There are .. of these waggons, the framing consists of iron with timber stays, and iron angles and brackets, plank flooring. Weighing in all about 2 ton 13 cwt and fitted with hand lever side brake, and centre sprung and buffers of carrying 6 ton. The wheel axel boxes, springs, framing and buffers of these waggons is in fair working order. In some instances, a rotten flooring or beam was noticeable as is also the want of paint generally. These remarks apply to the whole system of rolling stock.

"Low-sided waggons. Low side waggons with sides about 12 inches high. Of these, there are (blank) and are constructed in the same manner as the waggons previously described.

Their present condition is the same.

"High-sided waggons. High sided waggons weighing about 2 tons 16 cwt. (blank) of these.

"Covered vans. Covered vans, such as are used for perishable goods.

"Brake Vans. Brake vans or Guards' Vans. Vans fitted with hand brake to be worked from train.

"Travelling 5 ton Crane. Weighing machine, small hand cranes and 2 turntables , one of these is out of order - …

Further pages of this 1897 letter, completing the assessment of the line, are apparently no longer in existence.

Such was the parlous condition of the railway that the bondholders decided to take action. Their petition for winding up had been refused, and the application for further funds rejected. Faced with a seemingly impossible situation, they decided a full report on the railway was necessary and decided to consult another well-known light railway expert, Mr E.R Calthrop, of Barsi Light Railway (India) and Leek and Manifold Railway (England) fame.

The 2' 6" Era - a New Beginning for the Railway in Barbados

The Bridgetown and St.Andrews Railways Limited

Calthrop's choice of re-gauging the line to 2' 6" gauge comes as no surprise, as he had been a strong advocate of this gauge elsewhere, and had considerable expertise and experience of railways of this gauge in England and India. So, the new company set to and rapidly re-gauged the line. In 1897, the train service was curtailed, but, by 1898, a full service was restored.

The passenger stock was re-equipped with bogies, as recommended, and new locomotives were ordered, this time from the Baldwin Locomotive Works of Philadelphia, USA. Baldwin's had considerable experience of building narrow-gauge locomotives and the Barbadian examples were clearly from the same family of locomotives as those constructed for 2' 6"-gauge lines in Australia and South America, although the dimensions and wheel arrangements on those had been different.

The company's brave start was, alas, once again to be proved short-lived. The former Barbados Railway had enjoyed a government subsidy of some £6,000 per annum, a considerable operating subsidy at that time. Unfortunately for the new company, however, this luxury was no longer available, and what in fact had been the financial lifeline of the enterprise had been removed. The result was that throughout its short life the railway traded at a loss, and went into voluntary liquidation on 30 July 1903, just five years and two weeks after inception!

The Barbados Light Railway Company

The liquidator of the line ordered that it be closed on 15 October 1904. Unsuccessful attempts were made to rescue the company, but no buyers were found. This was despite an offer by the Barbados Government of an annual subsidy of £1,000, and an indication that the liquidator might be prepared to sell the entire railway for £10,000. A repair bill estimated to be in the order of some £6,500 no doubt did not assist the case. Finally, the Government stepped in and, after much debate, reluctantly proposed to increase the potential subsidy to £2,000 per annum.

In April 1905, a new company was set up, with the title of "The Barbados Light Railway Company Limited". This was another new dawn for the railway and this company set to and increased the timetable it operated. However, it was reported by the company in 1906 that virtually all the trains were so poorly patronised that they were all loss-making. Nevertheless, with the subsidy and receipts for freight traffic, together with a meagre income from passengers, the company struggled on through its first decade. Again, it experienced a mounting problem of unattended repairs through insufficient depreciation and lack of funds. In 1914, the Government subsidy was cut and, yet again, the railway's owners were forced into liquidation.

The Crane branch

During the company's short lifetime, it managed to extend the route system. Although the new company had been authorised to construct the extension to Speightstown, no work was ever carried out on it. Instead, in 1905, a branch line, some five miles in length, was constructed from Carrington station to The Crane. Very little is known of this branch, for it never carried passenger traffic. Indeed, advertisements for the Crane Hotel informed patrons of the availability of a buggy cart service from Bushy Park station, some distance away. It is assumed that the branch was solely for freight traffic.

Only two sources of reference to the Crane branch have been found during the compilation of this book. The first was in

A Swedish naval visit to Barbados in 1926, an example of the special excursion trains run for groups in the 1920s and 1930s.(BNT)

Baldwin Locomotives magazine, dated January 1930, where the branch is referred to in an article. Written by the Locomotive Superintendent of the Barbados Government Railway, Mr Willoughby Sayers, it reported that the line ran to the various sugar estates.

The second is a copy of an entry in The Barbados Diamond Jubilee Directory (year book) for 1905/6. This states that -

"A branch of about four miles from Carrington station to the Crane, which passes through many important sugar works, has recently been completed".

The Barbados Government Railway

At the end of 1915, the Barbados Government finally gave in and agreed to purchase the line, and, on 5 December 1916, the company passed into the Government's hands. Services were again interrupted while (yet more) much-needed repairs were undertaken. By 1917, services were able to be restored, with freight traffic resuming in February and passenger traffic in August.

Further problems

The line's problems were far from over and, indeed, the Government's take-over was eventually to prove to be the beginning of the line's final phase of existence. They bought a new locomotive from Baldwin's, gradually re-boilered the others, and converted them to oil-firing. However, all was not well with the finances of the line. Although surpluses were declared in 1920, 1922, 1923 and 1927, during the intervening years the railway traded at a loss, thus further draining Government revenues.

The table in Appendix 1 shows the railway's financial performance during its final decade.

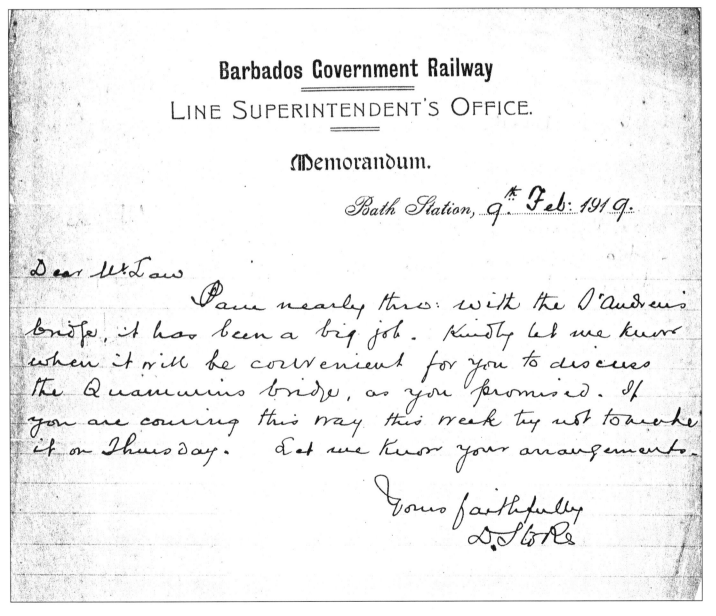

Memorandum referring to repair work on the Long Pond Bridge, illustrated on page 10. (PS)

Heading for trouble - The 1930s

The line continued to struggle on, with a declining set of assets and infrastructure. Incidents arising from insufficient maintenance and repair became more common, as there were simply no resources to fall back on to renew the railway. Derailments increased, and successive reports from inspectors and consulting engineers made ever-depressing reading.

On 6 August 1931, the Minutes by the Governor included the following:-

"I should like to have the views of the Board on the necessity for continuing maintenance of the Railway. Are there essential services rendered by the Railway which could not be performed if the railway were closed down?"

Printed on 5 September 1931, the following generally positive comments were made in reply by the Board:-

"How long can the Board carry on without extensive replacement of engines and materials?

"There is no immediate necessity for the replacement of locomotives, boilers, rolling stock or rails. The annual repairs and overhauling are sufficient to keep the existing plant as a going concern for some years.

"With the shops and mechanics at their disposal would it pay a Lorry and Bus service and abandon gradually rail transport?

"Owing to the lack of sufficient immediate funds (sic) for road transportation equipment the Board are not in a position on the substitution of road for rail transport, and would not hastily advise. The cost of running the dual system until the road transport is established would be very costly.

"The Board are of the opinion that it would be a retrograde step to abandon the railway.

"The question of the railway owning lorrys or making contact with lorry owners to act as feeders to the railway should be immediately considered.

"The convenience of the Factory owner should be given more consideration; his desire is for a door to door delivery; sufficient attention in the past has not been given to this matter, thus allowing privately owned lorrys to cater for the Factory, the result being the starving of railway and more traffic thrown on the roads.

"Now that the heavy type of lorry has been taken off the road, it is a grave question whether the small lorry travelling long distances could compete with the railway.

"The existing staff and mechanics would need to be trained for the special work of motor engineering, and many of the employees would be thrown out of work.

"The extra traffic on the roads both for passenger and freight should be duly considered looking to the fact that the permanent way of the railway is equipped with rails which will be serviceable for many years".

On 23 May 1933, the Governor of Barbados had the honour -

"...in compliance with the request contained in Resolution No. 6 which was forwarded with the Address from the Honourable the House of Assembly, dated 23rd May, 1933, to forward for the information of the Honourable House a copy of a report, dated 12th February, 1934, on the Railway by the Consulting Engineers".

The report, by Law and Connell, was addressed to C.L. Elder, Chairman of the Barbados Government Railway. The comments ranged from the now deplorable state of the track and trackbed to the lamentable state of the rolling stock, and the hopeless state of the buildings in Bridgetown. All the engines needed extensive repairs and overhaul.

Law and Connell are also reported to have advised that the bridge at Belle Gully was in need of such extensive repairs that passenger services over it were to be suspended until the work was done. So, the last passenger train from Belleplaine was the 4.20 p.m. departure on Saturday, 20 January 1934. The engineers who ordered the cessation of passenger traffic had already previously stepped in over the by now parlous state of the railway. In 1933, it had been reported that the railway had been forbidden to run a special train for tourists from a cruise ship on the grounds that it was unsafe to do so.

Yet again, an expert was brought over from England to assess the situation.

Mr. Gilling and his Report

The expert this time was Mr. A.H.Gilling, who set to and produced a thorough assessment of the railway. His task was not easy, for as he noted in his report -

"There are no details or plans of the concession granted to the Railway..."

He continued -

"There are no reliable plans of bridges, curves or grades nor of the Locomotives, Rolling Stock, equipment or buildings, no Inventory or Valuation of the Railway property exists nor information of any service regarding the cost and value of Plant and Machinery either original or present day. I understand that as no records were kept, or available, when the Government took over the Railway, it has not been considered necessary to make any change".

Perhaps the most notable feature of his report was his criticism, on page after page, of just about everything to do with the railway. However, his report was not solely negative. The overall message was that something must be done. The railway, he argued, must be operated in a more professional manner and be modernised with, amongst other things, diesel traction for its motive power. Otherwise, the railway will inevitably decline. His report summed up the locomotive fleet with the following statement:-

"I can only repeat that they are not worth repairing".

He considered that the only way that the railway could be effective was by serving much more of the island, thereby attracting far more of the available freight traffic. He suggested that branches be built to the many plantations not served by the railway, and that the line should be extended from St.Andrews to Speightstown, Holetown and back to Bridgetown. But, having costed this out at £2,500 per mile, he admitted that any extension to the system, or providing it with more modern equipment, was an unlikely possibility.

Meanwhile, the line itself continued to deteriorate. The section of route between Bathsheba and Belleplaine was closed to all traffic in May 1934 due to the state of the Long Pond Bridge.

Mr. Gilling's report was completed for the Railway Commission on 20 June 1934.

It was submitted to the Railway Commission, which had been established by the Governor of Barbados, on 20 August 1934. They set to and studied it carefully. The Commission's outcome was split, with two reports being submitted to the Governor, one by the majority of the Committee, presenting its Report, and the other one presenting a Minority Report.

The majority report concluded:

"Your Commissioners after carefully considering the evidence they have been able to procure are of the opinion that the Railway cannot be continued except at a loss, and as it is no longer fulfilling the object for which it was purchased by the Government, aided by the planters' contribution, they cannot recommend the continuance of a service which is no longer required by those for whose benefit it was purchased, nor even by those who contributed part of the purchase money".

The Commission further recommended that the sections of trackbed from Thicket to Bathsheba, and from Bathsheba to St.Andrews, be converted to roads.

However, they were mindful that if their conclusions were not proceeded with (i.e. should the line remain open), they recommended "that a qualified Railway Engineer should be appointed as General Manager directly responsible to the Governor-in-Executive Committee".

As mentioned above, some members of the Commission were of a different opinion, and produced a Minority Report, which took a far more conciliatory and almost optimistic view of the Railway's potential. They were keen that the railway be dieselised, or equipped with brand new, state-of-the-art steam locomotives, and that much of Mr. Gilling's proposals should be carried out.

Whilst the Commission's majority view to rid the Government of the liability was not proceeded with, neither was that of the minority. The latter's grandiose plans were to come to nothing.

Mr. Gilling's condemnation of the design of Long Pond Bridge was proved to be right, as a pier of the bridge was washed away in September 1936, and the span which it supported collapsed.

The line struggled to keep going, with freight traffic on the remaining section as far as Bathsheba continuing for another three years.

26th, 1931.

RAILWAY ACCIDENT

ENGINE DERAILED—PASSENGERS ESCAPED UNINJURED.

An unfortunate accident took place on Monday evening in connection with the passenger service of the Barbados Government Railway. The 4.15 p.m. passenger train pulled out from headquarters in Bridgetown for Belleplaine, two carriages being attached to the engine. All went well until Carrington factory was reached about 5 p.m. At this point through some cause which up to the present is baffling the authorities to discover, the engine jumped the main line and was derailed. The passengers quite naturally at once became scared but their fears were soon allayed by the action of the engine drivers who brought the engine to a standstill as promptly as possible and thus prevented a derailment of the carriages. As soon as information about the incident reached the Town Station a break-down engine was immediately despatched with workmen, materials and tools. Mr. C. A. Farmer, Acting Manager, and Mr. Clinckett, Traffic Manager, followed soon after and when they reached the scene of the accident their first consideration was to get the passengers to their respective homes as early as possible. Those who lived at great distances from the train stations in the Belleplaine, Bathsheba and Martins Bay districts were sent home in motor cars while the railway's trolleys conveyed others who lived not far away from the stations. Having been relieved of the anxiety of getting the passengers home, Mr. Farmer and his men turned their attention to replacing the engine on the line. This they succeeded in doing at a late hour in the night and the train continued its journey to Belleplaine under its own steam. The break-down engine returned to Bridgetown about 3 a.m. yesterday. No serious damage was done to the engine and happily none of the passengers or employees was injured.

Extract from a newspaper report of 26th August 1931 reporting an accident that had occurred on 24th August of that year. (PS)

A further Report, and the end of the railway

However impossible it may seem, conditions on the railway continued to deteriorate further. In 1937 yet another study was made, this time by Mr. E.M.Bland. His report was presented in February and March 1937. He concluded that time had run out for the railway, and that road transport could now cope far more effectively with the freight traffic (passenger traffic on the railway having already ceased in January 1934).

Among other gems, he reported that there was no longer a General Manager, the post being handled by the Secretary and Accountant. Neither was there any "Civil Engineer or Storekeeper, there being in fact no-one with any technical experience on the Railway".

The opening comments in his report to the Governor of Barbados included the following advice:-

"A report on the Railway was submitted by Mr. A. H. Gilling, M.I.C.E., in 1934, since when further deterioration has taken place though a few of the recommendations made by him have been carried out".

He continued -

"In dealing with the physical and other conditions I have the following comments to make. In the first place, no complete plans appear to exist nor could I find any reliable records showing the land originally acquired by the Railway though under clause 9.a. of the Railway Act, 1917, the Board is authorised to enter upon any land within 100 feet of the Railway for the purpose of properly maintaining the line".

Yet again, the lack of any records was highlighted.

Paragraph 99 of Mr. Bland's report (part of his detailed Recommendations) says it all:

"In arriving at my conclusions I wish to state that I was afforded the opportunity of meeting various Bodies and Associations representing the principal producers and merchants of the island. I visited one or two factories and in every case was supplied with the information asked for.

"I discussed the question with many people and with few exceptions (the latter never having been large shippers) all expressed the opinion that they carry on without the Railway.

"Having been directly connected with Railways all my life and during recent years opposed motor competition in every legitimate way, my sympathy is naturally with the older form of transport.

"I have endeavoured to find some means whereby the Barbados Railway might continue to serve the people of the Island, but am reluctantly forced to the conclusion that it has fulfilled its purpose and is no longer capable of being worked except at a heavy loss.

"In fact, everything points to the abandonment of the railway as the wisest and only course to adopt. The continuation of the service means heavy expenditure with absolutely no opportunity of obtaining sufficient revenue to balance out-goings.

"I recommend, therefore, that the early steps be taken to withdraw the present service and that the railway be definitely closed

as soon as possible".

This advice was readily accepted by the Government. The end was quick to follow. Later in 1937 the line closed, putting 106 employees out of work. On 12 October the Disposal Board authorised sale of the railway's assets and, in early 1938, contractors moved in and swiftly removed the track. Thus, the stricken little line succumbed to the inevitable and rapidly vanished from the scene.

After closure

The Government was keen to dispose of the railway and offered it for sale as a going concern. An Inventory of the items for sale was issued by the Secretary of the Railway Disposal Committee. This is illustrated in Appendix 3

In January 1938, the line was purchased by Mr. Morris Wexler, who was associated with Messrs. A. Gordon & Sons of Montreal, Canada. In Barbados, the manager of the Barbados Foundry, Mr. J.M. Kidney, was appointed their agent. He duly reported back that -

"The condition of the Railway is in such a state, that it is absolutely impossible to think of running it as a service. The Railway will definitely be scrapped.

"The iron will be shipped away, but the rails, carriages, and other materials will be sold locally.

"Mr. Wexler has bought the complete Railway, with the exception of the building and No.1 bridge which are retained by the Government".

More than 22 miles of track were sold as scrap iron for $20,000, and shipped abroad. The remainder of the rails were used in various construction projects on the island, or used as telegraph or electricity poles. Some of the latter lasted for many years.

The carriages were considered to be of sufficient condition to have further use, though not on a railway. Most were sold for use as accommodation at Lady Meade Gardens, opposite the General Hospital. In time, these were replaced by more permanent accommodation.

The first-class carriage suffered a different fate. Purchased by Mr. A.E. Taylor (who is reputed to have bought much else from the scrapped line, including some other coaches), it was converted into a small guest-house! It survived until the 1970s, when it succumbed to the elements and rotted away. The Barbados Daily News of 19 June 1967 featured an article about it and showed a photograph of the carriage, rotting away. The November 1975 edition of The Bajan also showed a photo of the coach, by now further rotting away. It really had an unfortunate fate, for if it had survived a little longer, no doubt it could have been rescued for the Barbados Museum.

The remains today

The earthworks of the line are virtually all that physically remain today. Memories of the line have been recorded, and the Barbados Museum has a commendable record and small collection of artefacts and photographs of the railway.

The only visible remains are the trackbed as one travels further out from Bridgetown. The site of the railway's terminus in Bridgetown was to become the market and Fairchild Street bus station. In the town's suburbs, the former trackbed becomes clearer, with low embankments and cuttings surviving as reminders of the old line.

Through the cane-fields east of Bridgetown, the line is still traceable, but fewer and fewer folk now remember it. It is only towards the Atlantic coast that the trackbed become obvious. Consett's Cutting remains, its steep grades being clear to the visitor today. It was clearly a folly and its attendant operational problems remain obvious.

Along the Atlantic coast itself, the former trackbed is clearly visible in many places. Several sections have been used in later years as roads, notably at Bath and Martin's Bay. North of Bathsheba, much of the trackbed from Cattlewash to Belleplaine is now the route of the Queen Elizabeth II Highway, opened in the late 1960s. Elsewhere on the coast, the earthworks of the line remain, a silent memorial to a charming little railway.

However, in the 1990s, a more tangible reminder of the railway was erected. On the northern end of the site of Bathsheba station, a café was built, and a commemorative plaque erected by the Barbados National Trust.

The café is called the Rail Road Café, and has a splendid Banks (beer of Barbados) name-board, alerting all visitors along the shore road in Bathsheba of its existence. The plaque reads as follows:-

"THE BARBADOS RAILWAY

On this site stood the Bathsheba Railway Station, a popular disembarkation spot for travelers (sic) on the Barbados Railway from Bridgetown to Belleplaine. A favourite pastime for the Bathsheba residents was to walk south to Tent Bay, and then return by train to this spot.

The Railway was originally built to facilitate the Sugar Industry. It was completed in 1883 and was privately operated until 1915, when it was taken over by the government.

The coal-fired steam locomotives were converted to oil after the end of World War I.

The Railway closed in 1937 due to increased competition from road traffic. Remnants of the tracks still exist between Martin's Bay and Belleplaine.

The Barbados National Trust

Sign donated by Foster and Ince Cruise Services Inc."

Occasionally, one comes across other reminders of the railway. For instance, there are still a number of tell-tale road names in Barbados. "Railway Road", "Train Line Road" and "Train Road" are obvious reminders of the past. The house next door to the renowned Atlantis Hotel in Bathsheba is still called "Train View".

But, as the years pass, memories of the railway inevitably dim as the numbers of folk who actually remember it become ever fewer.

Despite the undoubted dedication of the staff, at all levels in the Railway Company, as a functioning railway it failed miserably. Yet it played an important role in the development of Barbados and, in particular, the development of tourism on the Atlantic coast. It was hopelessly under-funded throughout its life, regardless of ownership, whether private or, later, publicly run, and was in all truth only able to survive for as long as it did thanks to the diligence and care given to it by its staff.

The Barbados Railway therefore deserves to be remembered - preferably, however, in the warmer hues of nostalgia rather than in the cooler light of economics.

The Route

No plans of the railway appear to have ever been produced! Accordingly, there are no details of track-plans, or layouts of the intermediate stations or sidings. Rather, the intermediate stations are only referred to in passing in the sources studied to produce this record.

Bridgetown

The line started in Bridgetown at a terminus east of the Careenage and on the south side of the Constitution River. There was, however, an extension of the line seawards. It ran along Fairchild Street, crossing the mule-tram lines in Bay Street and on into Pier Head Lane. It then continued out alongside the Careenage to facilitate loading from the quayside onto the lighters which then conveyed the freight out to the ships waiting in deep water. From photographic records, there was a run-round loop at the seawards end of the branch, and reference is made to it crossing Probyn Street through a triangle of land on a photograph illustrated in the book "Barbados Yesterday and Today".

A panoramic view of the station and its surroundings forms the frontispiece to the Guide to Barbados, published in 1913. This photo clearly shows the gates and the seaward end of the station, with the line extending onwards across The Triangle.

CAREENAGE, BARBADOS.

A very early postcard view of the Careenage, showing the railway sidings. (DJH)

An early general view card of Bridgetown, showing the Careenage and Railway (top), and street scenes, including the Bridgetown mule tramcars (centre), and further views of the Careenage. (DJH)

The road crossing of this seaward extension, beyond the station, was protected by gates. Not that they were much use, however, as on a few occasions trains burst through them, across The Triangle, and headed off towards the wharf. When the extension was taken out of use, the line, now terminating within the station area, was fitted with a rudimentary buffer by means of heating the rails and bending them two feet into the air! The line was probably taken out of use in the 1920s. Mr. Gilling proposed its reinstatement and, further, suggested that if a deep-water harbour was ever built, then the railway should extend there too,

General view of Bridgetown station. (DJH)

Below: The course of the line from the Careenage to Rouen Station. (DJH)

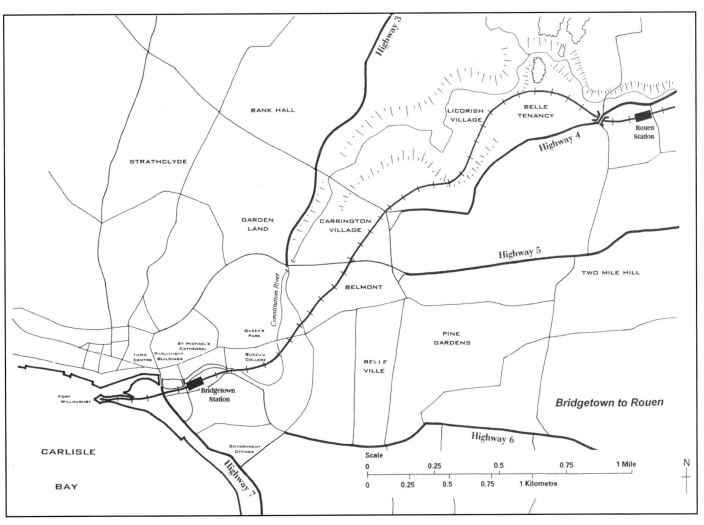

Bridgetown 1890 - the Careenage inner basin, showing sailing ships, lighters and, on the quayside branch line, flat wagons loaded with puncheons and some covered vans transhipping freight for export. (BNT)

Bridgetown Roundhouse, showing two Baldwin tank locomotives and a 'Galloping Goose' type rail motor. (DJH)

Bridgetown station with freight loading for the Careenage? (DJH)

in order to afford direct transhipment from train to ship. The idea of the reinstatement of the extension was dismissed out of hand by the 1934 Railway Commission.

Bridgetown was the railway's principal station. Initially, when the line was constructed, photographs of the period show a single-storey building. However, records show that, afterwards, a two-storey main station building was constructed, containing various offices, with two platform faces. Along one side, there lay one of the through-lines of the station yard (leading to the line to the Careenage?). On the other side (the road side), there was a siding in a bay. The platform was covered with a long canopy along the station building and extending a distance beyond, along the bay platform. It was constructed of wood, with a large, curved, corrugated iron roof. Along the platform side of the station, there was a first-floor balcony fronted with appropriate and typical tropical shutters.

The station building contained the booking hall and office, and the Traffic and Line Superintendent's office. There was also what is referred to as the "Sugar Warehouse" (the roof of which came in for much criticism in several reports).

There were other buildings at Bridgetown terminus.

The locomotive shed was a roundhouse (unfortunately, no record of the number of stalls it contained seems to exist). A photograph in an edition of the Baldwin Magazine suggests that it was not very large. Since the fleet comprised only five locomotives, it is likely that the roundhouse was designed to accommodate a roster of about that size (one locomotive was out-stationed at St.Andrew's shed). It is understood that the rolling stock was repaired in one bay of the roundhouse. Both Mr. Gilling's and Mr. Bland's reports commented on the appalling state of repair of the Bridgetown roundhouse. It had long lost a watertight roof.

A rare early photo taken during the excavations for the Bridgetown terminus. The locomotive shown is the contractor's 0-4-0T 'St. Michael'. (DB)

Indeed, the roof (made of corrugated iron, like so many of the railway's buildings), was so corroded, it afforded no protection from the weather.

There were several small stores, a smithy, a foundry, a machine shop and a locomotive repair shop. A photograph has come to light of the railway's somewhat simple and basic workshop. Whilst repairs to rolling stock were done under cover in the roundhouse, space there accommodated only one coach at a time, in a area so tight that external repairs, painting, etc. had to be done in the open air.

There was a small carriage shed which, from photographs, appears to have had only one line in it, which extended out beyond the other end.

A view of Bridgetown Station with one of the 1898 2ft-6in gauge Baldwin 2-8-2Ts making a stormy departure. (DJH)

RIVER ROAD BRIDGE SHOWING BARBADOS RAILWAY. BARBADOS. B.W.I.

View of a 2ft-6in gauge train heading out of Bridgetown across the Constitution River. This is one of the best illustrations of the Baldwin 2-8-2Ts shown on a postcard. (DB)

Below: An Avonside 2-4-0 in the workshops, Bridgetown. The date is unknown, probably in the 1880s. (BNT)

From the reports made in the 1930s, there appears to have been a general air of decay at the terminus. Mr. Gilling makes reference to extensive clutter and junk, and to a 6ft high dump of refuse which must have added to the squalid atmosphere of the place.

From the Fairchild Street terminus, the line headed eastwards, crossing twice over the Constitution River before turning northeastwards through the eastern suburbs of the town.

East of Bridgetown - Rouen to Three Houses

The line climbed up gradually out of Bridgetown, towards the interior of the island. In this part of the island, it crossed a long, level plateau between hills to the north and a sharp drop down to the southern sea coast. East of Bridgetown, the first station reached was Rouen, some two and a half miles from the terminus. This was located just before the start of sugar-cane country, south

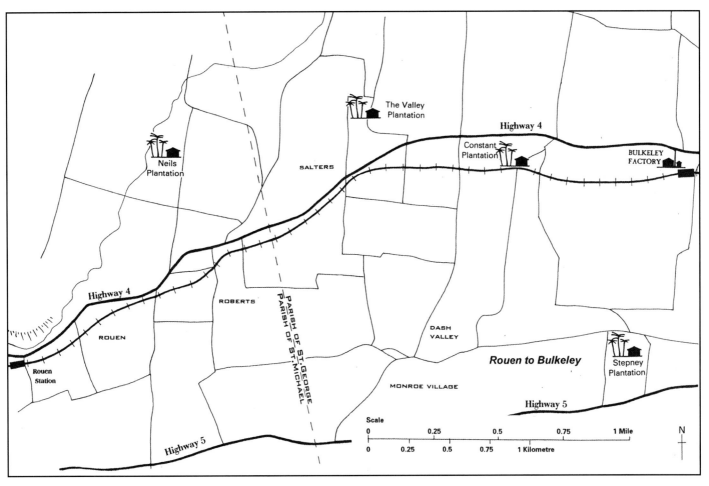

Neils Plantation

The Valley Plantation

SALTERS

Highway 4

Constant Plantation

BULKELEY FACTORY

Highway 4

ROBERTS

PARISH OF ST.GEORGE
PARISH OF ST.MICHAEL

DASH VALLEY

ROUEN

Rouen Station

MONROE VILLAGE

Rouen to Bulkeley

Stepney Plantation

Highway 5

Scale

| 0 | 0.25 | 0.5 | 0.75 | 1 Mile |

| 0 | 0.25 | 0.5 | 0.75 | 1 Kilometre |

Highway 5

N

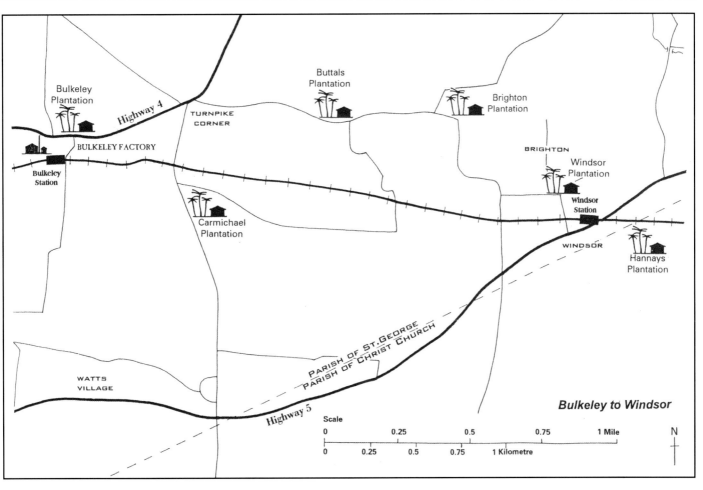

Bulkeley Plantation

Highway 4

TURNPIKE CORNER

Buttals Plantation

Brighton Plantation

BRIGHTON

BULKELEY FACTORY

Bulkeley Station

Windsor Plantation

Windsor Station

WINDSOR

Carmichael Plantation

Hannays Plantation

PARISH OF ST.GEORGE
PARISH OF CHRIST CHURCH

WATTS VILLAGE

Highway 5

Bulkeley to Windsor

Scale

| 0 | 0.25 | 0.5 | 0.75 | 1 Mile |

| 0 | 0.25 | 0.5 | 0.75 | 1 Kilometre |

N

Bulkeley Station, St. George. Note the hand crane and, beyond it, a field of sugar cane. (BNT)

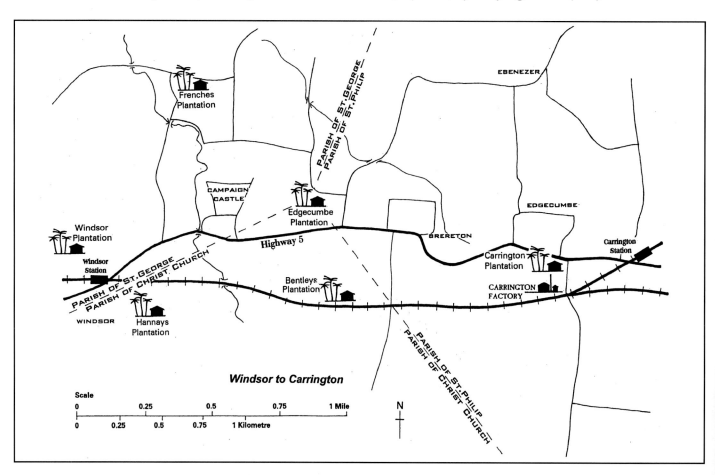

Two views of a train at Carrington Station. The top photo is slightly distorted but shows in the loop a couple of flat wagons, while off the track is a handcart and the obligatory grazing livestock, unmoved by the passage of the train. In the lower photo we see locomotive no. 1 at the head of the train taking water. (BNT)

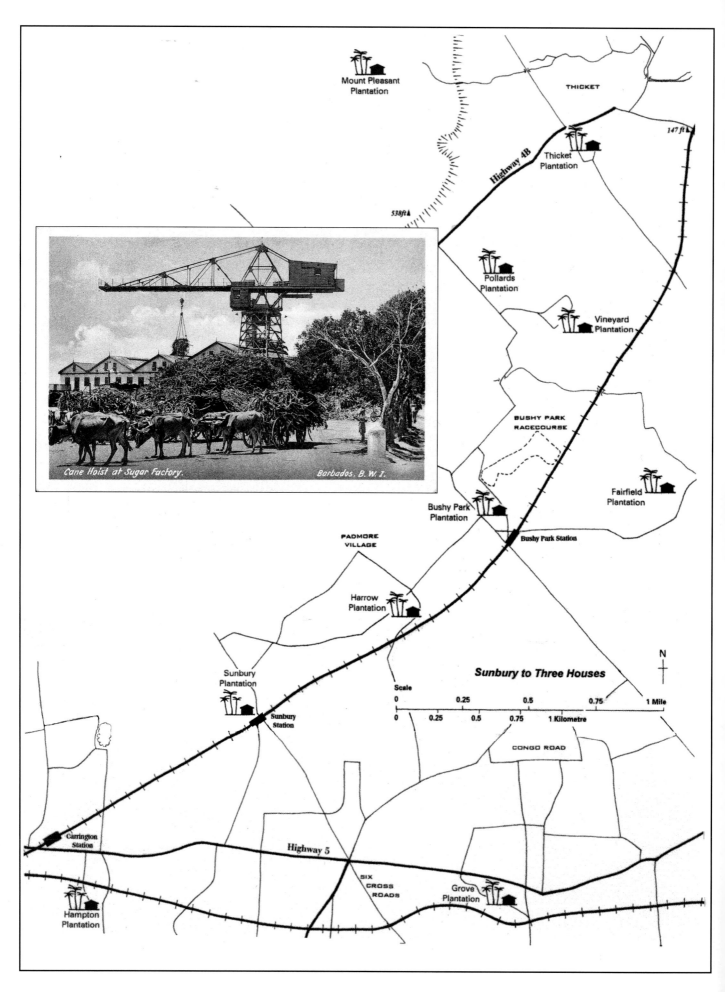

Mount Pleasant Plantation

THICKET

Highway 4B

Thicket Plantation

147 ft

538 ft

Pollards Plantation

Vineyard Plantation

BUSHY PARK RACECOURSE

Fairfield Plantation

Cane Hoist at Sugar Factory.   Barbados, B.W.I.

Bushy Park Plantation

Bushy Park Station

PADMORE VILLAGE

Harrow Plantation

N

Sunbury Plantation

Sunbury to Three Houses

Scale

0   0.25   0.5   0.75   1 Mile

Sunbury Station

0   0.25   0.5   0.75   1 Kilometre

CONGO ROAD

Carrington Station

Highway 5

SIX CROSS ROADS

Grove Plantation

Hampton Plantation

of today's Highway 4. From here the line ran virtually due east, through the gently undulating cane-fields, for the next ten miles.

After Rouen, the next station was at the sugar factory of Bulkeley, five and a half miles from Bridgetown. A photograph of Bulkeley (pronounced "Buckley") station building shows a basic, small waiting room. Whether this was the only station building here, or is just a small additional waiting room is not known. No known photographs have come to light of Rouen or Windsor stations, the next station seven miles out, and where the line crossed Highway 5. A photograph has materialised which could have been taken at Windsor, but there are no identifiable indicators that this is actually the case, except that the general layout of the station buildings suggest that it could have been photographed from the station level crossing. Until such evidence confirms their track layouts, it can only be assumed that there were passing loops at these stations, and that at the sugar factories en route there were likely to have been some sidings to load the sugar products.

The sugar factories were at Bulkeley, Carrington and Three Houses. The author remembers seeing a small sugar cane wagon preserved in the grounds of Sunbury House, adjacent to the former trackbed. The house contained a set of railway photographs in its cellar kitchens, which survive today.

Reports in the November 1975 edition of The Bajan magazine suggest that there were only three sugar factories which used rail transport. The Bajan notes that the canes were packed into the open wagons by hand, before being transported by train to the three factories. This suggests that the cane was loaded at the cane-fields along the line, prior to shipment to the factories. At the factories themselves, the cane was manually unloaded from the wagons. It appears that if the trains were entirely composed of cane wagons, then the locomotive would run round, and propel the train into the factory's sidings. However, if the train also carried passengers or other freight traffic, then often the wagons were just set down in the station loops.

A photograph of Bridgetown station shows a four-wheeled open cane wagon on a siding (presumably there for repairs, as the cane itself was not transported down the line to the capital).

The next station was Carrington, nine miles out. There have been photographs taken here, which have survived over the years. Some are of obvious questionable quality, but are included for sake of completeness. They show two passing loops and at least one siding, while photographs of Carrington Sugar Factory also show railway tracks around the factory site. The station building was single-storied, with match-boarding sides and a sloping roof which fell away from the trackside towards the rear. Along the front was a canopy, supported from the building by curved brackets. One photograph suggests that the building was constructed in three adjoining sections, the canopy attached to the centre one. Two photographs illustrated showing Carrington are confirmed by the existence of a large water tank known to have been located here at one end of the platform. Carrington became the junction for the branch-line to the Crane, opened in 1905, but records and details of this are even scarcer than those of the main line. There are reports of a severe curve in the vicinity of Carrington, which apparently caused operating problems (i.e. derailments) on occasions.

After Carrington, the main line turned north-eastwards and passed through Sunbury, another sugar factory and plantation, ten miles from town, and on to Bushy Park, the next station, eleven miles out. Continuing through predominantly cane-fields, the line then turned almost due north and headed for Three Houses station, located at another sugar factory. This station was thirteen miles from Bridgetown.

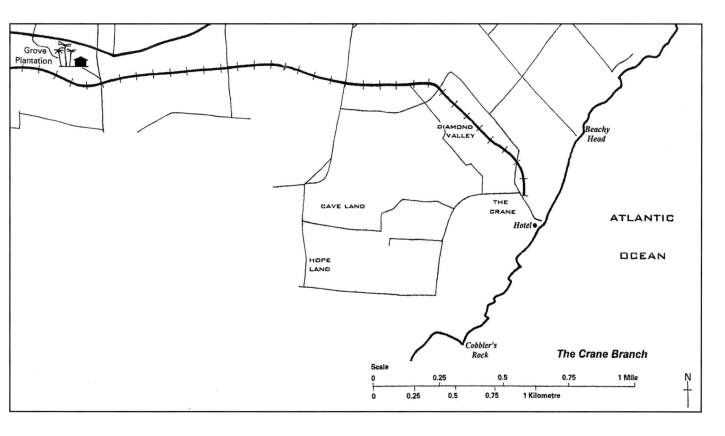

Three Houses to the Atlantic coast

North of Three Houses the landscape and character of the line changed. The cane-fields petered out, as the land becomes more exposed to the Atlantic winds. The land hereabouts is some 150 feet above sea level, on the eastern edges of the plateau, and drops down steeply to sea level, with only a narrow edge of land along the coast all the way up to Bathsheba and beyond.

The railway, as built, had to cope with this considerable change in levels. As previously mentioned, the contractor had revised the route and had chosen to gain access to the coast by the construction of a steeply-graded alignment, descending through

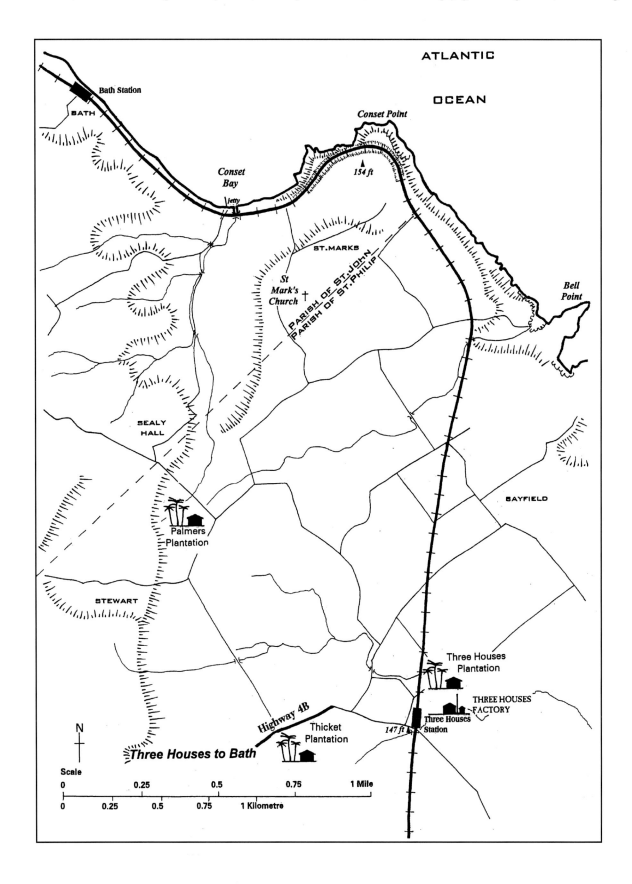

the solid rock down to Consett Bay - through Consett's Cutting. The impact that this section of route had on operations has already been referred to. It proved to be a problem for the railway throughout its existence. On numerous occasions, trains slipped to a standstill when trying to ascend Consett's Cutting. On one occasion, when a freight train of open trucks loaded with molasses was ascending the bank, the last three trucks broke loose from the train and gathered speed as they accelerated down the gradient. Unfortunately, there were three youngsters stealing a ride on one of these wagons. One managed to jump off. One, on the landward side, escaped with some severe cuts and bruises from the cutting's rock walls, but the last one tragically was on the seaward side of the wagon, and, on jumping off, managed to impale himself on an old rail now used on the railway's sea defences. The runaway trucks carried on over a mile beyond College Savannah, through Consett Bay, stopping finally near Bath station.

Right: Consett's Cutting in 1883, showing the contractor's 0-4-0T. Noteworthy is the lightweight track and the heavy gradient upwards behind the locomotive. (DJH)

A view of the east coast, looking northwards. The railway is just emerging from Consett's Cutting and heading down to the coast, to continue northwards to Belleplaine. (DJH)

An early view of the line emerging from Consett's Cutting, though still clearly at an incline. (BMHS)

The bottom of the incline at Consett's Bay, where the railway reaches the Atlantic coast. (BMHS)

The Atlantic coast - Consett Bay to Belleplaine

This was the section of route that both kept the line going and also assisted its eventual downfall. The contribution to its survival was in the numbers of tourists who used the trains to reach this beautiful part of the island, for this coastline was justly famed for its tourist potential. However, it was on unstable land where the railway track-bed was difficult to maintain. This area was very exposed to extremes of damp weather, both from the skies and from the sea, corroding the rails, thus further exacerbating the problems.

There were three stations on this part of the route. These were, in fact, only the official stopping places, as trains stopped elsewhere en route, as will be explained later. The first station was at the village of Bath, sixteen miles from the terminus, which boasted a passing loop and at least one siding. There are several published photographs of this station, the appearance of which changed over the years. In the early 1900s, the station had a tiny shelter, but later photographs show it replaced by a more substantial one, a station building with a canopy. As at Carrington, there was a raised, rectangular water tank at the Bridgetown end of the station.

A postcard view of Bath Station. Note the haphazard manner of loading barrels on the wagon on the right! (DJH)

BATH STATION, BARBADOS.

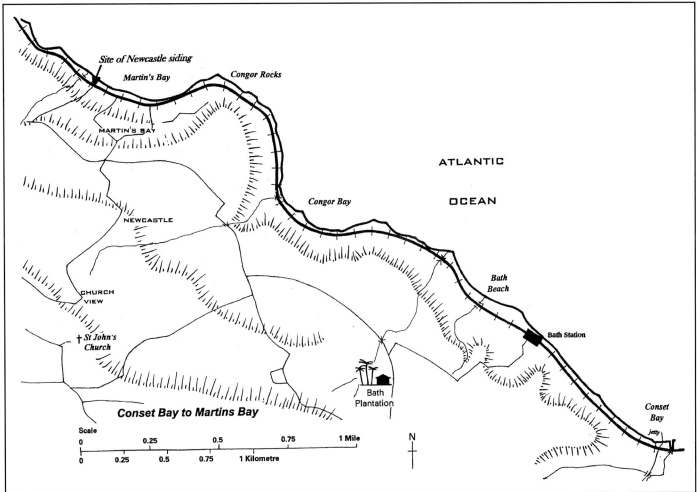

The station building at Bath survives to this day. Supported on tar-covered ex-railway carriage chasses, the building is now used as a rural retreat by the Simpson family.

(This section of the island's coast has long been a major tourist attraction, and so, over the years, has been the subject of numer-ous picture postcards. These have assisted in determining the layouts and nature of both Bath and Bathsheba stations. Elsewhere on Barbados, alas, photographs are rarer, so confirming station layouts has proved well nigh impossible).

From Bath to Bathsheba, the line hugs the coast, passing bays,

Bathsheba Coast, Barbados, B. W. I.

small beaches, groves of palm trees, and several dramatic rock outcrops in the turbulent waters of the Atlantic. This coastal area was banana country, with acres of the crop on the tumbling hillsides sloping down to the coastline.

Along this section of line were at least two sidings. The first one was located in Martins Bay, and was known as Newcastle siding. This was sited just south of a river bridge in Martins Bay, at the end of a track down from Newcastle Estate itself.

The second one was near Three Boys Rocks, and was known as Foster Hall siding, so named after the neighbouring estate.

Before reaching Bathsheba, the train also stopped at Martin's Bay. Here, alongside the single line, there was a rudimentary hut,

This photo showing the rudimentary halt at Martins Bay was used for a postcard published prior to 1922. (DJH)

A postcard view of the southern approach of the line at Bathsheba; the balconied building to the left of the line is the famed Atlantis Hotel. (DJH)

Bathsheba, Barbados, British West Indies.—24856.

which is visible on an old view.

On approaching Bathsheba, the train often called at the Atlantis Hotel, at Tent Bay, before continuing around the headland into Bathsheba station. At Bathsheba, there was a freight siding in the form of a loop through a goods' shed. Like several of the railway's buildings, the shed's construction and appearance varied over time, as there are several versions of it illustrated on local postcards. Bathsheba station was twenty miles from

Bridgetown by rail (but, alas, only thirteen by road - this, however, was not a problem until the roads were improved, when road transport then began to make an impact on the line).

At some time around 1920, a passenger carriage was mounted on blocks jutting out of a rocky slope down to the sea. This was immediately to the north of Bathsheba station, and was used as a shelter for visitors picnicking in Bathsheba. It was colloquially known as the "Rest House".

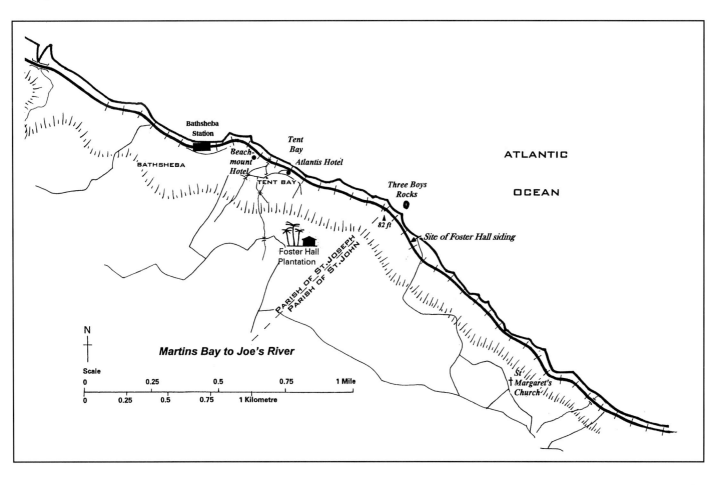

Locomotive no. 1 at the head of an excursion train at Tent Bay, Bathsheba, in the early 1930s. (FJH)

Atlantis Hotel
Bathsheba
Barbados

A charming sea-side resort.

Train stops at the foot of the door-steps.

J. R. Bryden & Co., Ltd., Barbados.

The Atlantis Hotel, Bathsheba. (DJH)

BARBADOS BATHSHEBA   Nr. 17.

Another view of the Atlantis Hotel, seen again from the track-bed, but looking back in the opposite direction. (DJH)

Atlantic Hotel, Bathsheba, Barbados.

COLLINS & CO. COPYRIGHTED.

In the middle distance a train stands outside the Atlantis Hotel. Note that the train is propelling a flat wagon ahead of the locomotive, probably pushed from Bath and destined for Bathsheba station goods loop.
(Note also the mis-spelling of Atlantis as 'Atlantic' on this postcard). (DJH)

Atlantis Hotel, Barbados.

This postcard view of the trackbed at Tent Bay is undated, but a message on the reverse was written on 3rd January 1939. (DJH)

A Bridgetown-bound train enters the station behind one Baldwin 2-8-2 tank no. 1. Note the carriage body known as the 'Rest House' mounted on blocks to the left of the station. (From 'Barbados Yesterday & Today')

Right: this similar view is on a postcard postmarked 14th August 1914. Note there is no goods shed at all at this time, nor has the 'Rest House' been installed yet. (DJH)

BATHSHEBA STATION, BARBADOS.

Below: An enlargement of part of a postcard view of Bathsheba clearly showing the carriage mounted on blocks and used as a shelter. (DJH)

A Belleplaine-bound train leaves a crowd of alighted passengers and attendant train greeters at Bathsheba station. (DJH)

A view looking south into Bathsheba station; on the right, the goods shed and, dominating the hill above, the Beachmount Hotel, which later burnt down. (DJH)

Beyond Bathsheba

Beyond Bathsheba were a series of large houses which were built for visiting tourists. These included Powell Springs, Edgewater and Tenby. Often, the train would stop at these houses, by request of the guests staying there.

(Powell Springs was regularly rented by the author's grand-parents during summers in the early 20th century, and on into the 1920s and 1930s. They frequently stopped the train directly outside the house).

Beyond these holiday homes lay Joe's River, which was crossed by a large (by Barbados Railway standards) bridge. It had brick abutments at each end, supplemented by two large intermediate brick piers; the track was supported on wooden trestles. Mention is made of a siding here, too, but only one photograph,

believed to have been taken there, has been traced, of a special excursion train alongside a small siding on the left-hand side of the track, facing Bridgetown. The layout of the trackwork in the photograph suggests that the siding lay on the Cattlewash (i.e. northern side) of Joe's River bridge.

North of Joe's River, the line continued to skirt the coastline through Cattlewash onwards to the terminus. In parts, the coastal plain here was wider, but it narrowed below a large cliff under Chalky Mount, about a mile before Belleplaine. Located between Cattlewash (so named because, to this day, the cattle are walked into the sea to be washed here) and Chalky Mount, was the 15-acre Barclays Park, donated to the Government for the public's use by Barclays Bank International. Again, although there was no station, the trains often stopped here as it was a popular picnic spot.

Looking back to Bathsheba station (in the middle distance). Note how the station has acquired a goods shed over the freight siding to the right of the main running line. (DJH)

A view further along the railway line towards the north west. Standing on the track presents no danger to the people here. (DJH)

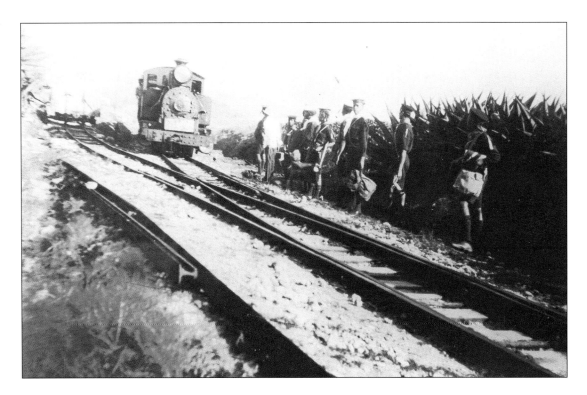

A Bridgetown-bound train at Joe's River siding, about to pick up a group of Sea Scouts. (Photo: property of the First Barbados Sea Scouts).

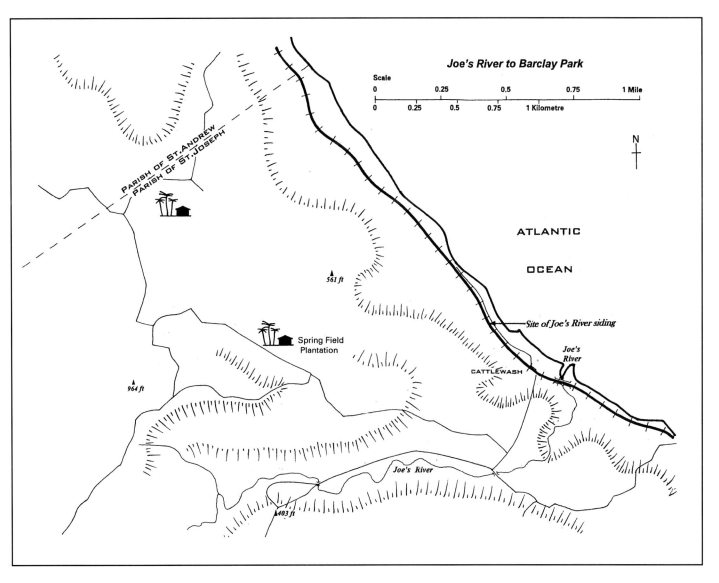

Joes River Bridge, Barbados

A postcard of Joe's River Bridge.
(DJH)

JOES RIVER, BATHSHEBA, BARBADOS.

Postcard view of a Belleplaine-bound train hauled by the smaller Baldwin tank locomotive on Joe's River Bridge.
The original photo was not very clear and had been touched up for reproduction on the card. (MK)

Beyond Chalky Mount, the line turned inland into Belleplaine. After crossing Long Pond Bridge (the collapse of which in September 1936 caused the closure of the line beyond Bathsheba), the line entered the outskirts of that hamlet, some twenty-four miles from Bridgetown. It was truly in the "middle of nowhere". It was the terminus of the line because, firstly, it petered out there, and, secondly, it was surrounded by chalky hills that would have proved very difficult for the railway to surmount. Thus, having ended up in a virtual cul-de-sac, the line had nowhere else to go easily - and, in any event, nobody had any money to get it there.

The railway always called Belleplaine station "St.Andrew's" station (after the parish where it was located). It had a small locomotive shed (one was stabled here overnight because of the nature of the timetable), a turntable and, no doubt, some sidings. Reports indicate that like many buildings on the line, the engine shed was in a dire state of repair towards the end of the railway's life, and needed new doors, roof and repairs to its walls! Parts of the station building still remains, used today as a sports pavilion, with the station's track-bed now forming part of a sports field.

Belleplaine itself is surrounded by palm-fringed hills. It is a truly beautiful spot, but one cannot help wondering why the railway ever came here.

Left: a Bridgetown-bound train passing Tenby behind Baldwin 2-8-2T No. 2. (DB)

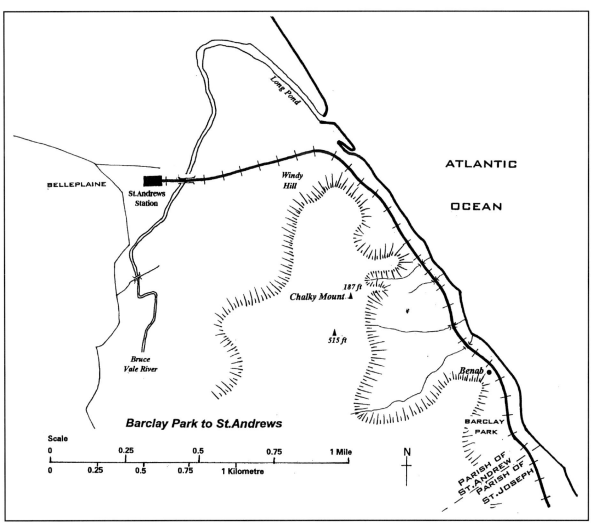

An excursion train, hauled by Baldwin 2-8-2T no. 2, collects picnickers at Barclays Park. (DB)

St. Andrew's Station, Belleplaine. The lady in the front seat is Agnes Horsford, with her daughter Gwen behind. (BMHS)

Train Services

There was never an intensive train service on the Barbados Railway, and finding examples of timetables has proved a considerable exercise.

The initial service (which ran for only a few days in October 1881 before being suspended) was between Bridgetown and Carrington. It is reported as being two return journeys per day, presumably two out-and-back journeys from Bridgetown. According to Lt. Col. Peter Tamlyn in his "Short History of the Crane", the train left Bridgetown at 8.00 a.m. with the journey taking 40 minutes, returning to Bridgetown at 9.00 a.m. In the afternoon, the train left at 4.00 p.m. and (presumably) returned at 5.00 p.m., although this last timing is not specified by Lt. Col. Tamlyn.

When the service resumed in December, three return journeys were operated. The Herald noted in 1894 that there was a local service within the confines of Bridgetown operated by the smallest tank locomotive and a double-deck carriage converted from a sugar wagon. How long this service lasted is not recorded.

The timetable of The Bridgetown and St.Andrew's Railways Ltd is not known but, by 1910, The Barbados Light Railway Co. Ltd. had increased the service. This consisted of a return trip daily from Belleplaine to Bridgetown and back (7.40 a.m. into town, 4.30 p.m. return), with an additional train from Bridgetown on Sundays, Tuesdays, Thursdays and Saturdays, returning from Belleplaine in the evenings. The timetable for 1910 was short-lived, but is shown here (*left*).

The railway's timetable seems to have settled pretty much into a set pattern, as the island's guidebook for 1912 printed a very similar one (*reproduced overleaf*).

That of 3 April 1922 suggested a slight variation, in that the daytime excursion from Bridgetown to St. Andrew's ran on Sundays and Wednesdays. The daytime service into Bridgetown seems unclear from this timetable, the days of operation having been crossed out by hand.

It is known, however, that other trains ran, by arrangement with the railway company, particularly for the passengers of visiting cruise ships.

BARBADOS LIGHT RAILWAY
Manager: G. V. de la Bastide, C.E.

Passenger Train Service—August 2, 1910, and until further notice.

| Miles from Bridgetown | OUTWARD TRAINS | | | | INWARD TRAINS | | | |
	Stations	Daily Except Sundays	Extra on Wednesdays only	Sundays	Stations	Daily Except Sundays	Extra on Wednesdays only	Sundays
		P.M.	A.M.	A.M.		A.M.	P.M.	P.M.
	Bridgetown .	4.30	7.45	7.40	St. Andrew's .	7.40	4.20	7.10
2½	Rouen .	4.43	7.57	7.52	Bathsheba .	8.00	4.40	7.30
5½	Bulkeley .	4.55	8.10	8.05	Bath . .	8.20	5.00	7.50
7	Windsor .	5.02	8.17	8.12	Three Houses .	8.33	5.15	8.05
9	Carrington {a	5.09	8.25	8.19	Bushy Park {a	8.41	5.22	8.12
	{d	5.13	8.29	8.23	{d	8.44	5.24	8.15
10	Sunbury .	5.18	8.34	8.28	Sunbury .	8.49	5.29	8.19
11	Bushy Park {a	5.23	8.39	8.33	Carrington {a	8.53	5.33	8.23
	{d	5.26	8.42	8.35	{d	8.57	5.37	8.27
13	Three Houses .	5.36	8.51	8.43	Windsor .	9.04	5.44	8.34
16	Bath . .	5.50	9.05	8.56	Bulkeley .	9.11	5.51	8.41
20	Bathsheba .	6.10	9.25	9.15	Rouen . .	9.23	6.03	8.53
24	St. Andrew's .	6.30	9.45	9.35	Bridgetown .	9.35	6.15	9.05

Same Day Return Trips from Bridgetown to Bathsheba, etc., can be made on Sundays and Wednesdays.

Combined rail and hotel tickets issued. Special tourists' excursions arranged.

The company will not be liable for failure to convey passengers from or to any places other than stations, and all tickets, single or return, are issued on these conditions.

Table of Passenger Fares
Through Fares from and to Bridgetown :

Miles from Bridgetown	Stations and Halts					First Class	Third Class
						Cents	Cents
2½	Rouen .	.	.	.	.	6	4
5½	Bulkeley .	.	.	.	.	12	6
7	Windsor .	.	.	.	.	18	8
9	Carrington	.	.	.	.	24	12
10	Sunbury .	.	.	.	.	30	14
11	Bushy Park	.	.	.	.	36	16
13	Three Houses .	.	.	.	.	42	16
16	Bath .	.	.	.	.	48	20
20	Bathsheba .	.	.	.	.	60	24
24	St. Andrew's .	.	.	.	.	60	24

Local Fares per Section :

| First Class | . | . | 6 c. | Maximum Fare | . | 60 c. |
| Third " | . | . | 2 c. | " " | . | 24 c. |

BARBADOS LIGHT RAILWAY.

PASSENGER TRAIN SERVICE.

Miles from Bridgetown.	OUTWARD TRAINS.				INWARD TRAINS.			
	STATIONS	DAILY Except Sundays.	Extra on Wednesdays only.	Sundays.	STATIONS.	DAILY Except Sundays.	Extra on Wednesdays only.	Sundays.
		P.M.	A.M.	A.M		A.M.	P.M.	P.M
	Bridgetown	4.30	7.45	7.40	St. Andrew's	7.40	4.20	7.10
2½	Rouen ...	4.43	7.57	7.52	Bathsheba ...	8.00	4.40	7.30
5½	Bulkeley ...	4 55	8.10	8.05	Bath ...	8.20	5.00	7.50
7	Windsor ...	5.02	8.17	8.12	Three Houses	8.33	5.15	8.05
9	Carrington {a	5.09	8.25	8.19	B Park {a	8.41	5.22	8.12
	{d	5.13	8.29	8.23	{d	8.44	5.24	8.15
10	Sunbury ..	5 18	8.34	8.28	Sunbury ...	8.49	5.29	8.19
11	B Park {a	5.23	8.39	8.33	Carrington {a	8.53	5.33	8.23
	{d	5.26	8.42	8.35	{d	8.57	5.37	8.27
13	Three Houses	5 36	8.51	8.43	Windsor. ...	9.04	5.44	8.34
16	Bath ...	5.50	9.05	8.56	Bulkeley ...	9.11	5.51.	8.41
20	Bathsheba ..	6.10	9.25	9.15	Rouen ...	9.23	6.03	8.53
24	St. Andrew's	6.30	9.45	9.35	Bridgetown	9.35	6.15	9.05

Fares

In 1905, the Diamond Jubilee yearbook advertised the fares as follows:

To or from Bridgetown from -

	1st class	3rd class
Rouen	6 cents	3 cents
Bulkeley	12 cents	6 cents
Windsor	24 cents	8 cents
Carrington	24 cents	12 cents
Sunbury	24 cents	14 cents
Bushy Park	32 cents	16 cents
Three Houses	36 cents	16 cents
Bath	36 cents	18 cents
Bathsheba	48 cents	24 cents
St. Andrew's	48 cents	24 cents

The last known fares information was released in 1929. They were approximately one penny per mile first class and one half-penny per mile third class. Reductions were available "in cases of school children, teachers, picnic parties, excursionists and others".

Return fares were three-quarters of two single fares.

In the 1930s, these fares compared poorly with the railway's rival, the bus. Fares between Bridgetown, Bathsheba and St.Andrew's were as follows:-

- to Bathsheba:
  - by rail   1st class 2/-
                    3rd class 9d
  - by bus   9d to 1/-

- to St.Andrew's:
  - by rail   1st class 2/-
                    3rd class 1/-
  - by bus   9d to 1/-

The Locomotives

As with all records to do with this railway, determining facts about the rolling stock generally has taken some detection, though finding details of the locomotives proved somewhat easier than the other rolling stock. When dealing with scant information, particularly relying on uncertain records dating back to the 19th century, some assumptions have inevitably had to be made but, wherever possible, the factual situation has tried to be established.

The 3' 6"-gauge locomotives

The first loco to be used on the line was owned by the contractor building the line. It was a saddle tank loco, an 0-4-0T, Black, Hawthorn no.575, called "St Michael". The author has an indistinct copy of a photo showing this loco, with the inscription on the reverse reading "...first train over Belle Gully bridge, 1880", and it appears on other photographs included in this book.

This loco was taken into capital stock by the company and, indeed, was apparently used on the Bridgetown local service referred to previously, and assumed to have become No.5 in the railway's numbering scheme. It is reputed to have survived until the gauge changeover in 1898.

The locomotives constructed for the opening of the line were a decidedly mixed bunch. The first two, built by the Avonside Engine Company of Bristol, were 2-4-0 locomotives, with four-wheel tenders. Several good photographs exist of these locomotives, and a fair representative drawing was printed in The Graphic.

These locomotives were unsuitable for the line, being underpowered for the steep, long climb from the Atlantic coast up to the inland plains. Some photographs show them at the head of freight trains, but in all likelihood, their haulage abilities were limited.

No.1 Avonside Engine Company 1286 1881/2 2-4-0
No.2 Avonside Engine Company 1287 1881/2 2-4-0

The other two early locomotives were more suited to the line. They were:-
No.3 Vulcan Foundry (Lancashire) 951/1882 2-6-2T
No.4 Vulcan Foundry (Lancashire) 952/1882 2-6-2T

The above had the following names:-
No. 1 St.John
No. 2 St.Joseph
No. 3 St.George
No. 4 Christchurch

In the light of the inadequacies of some of the initial locomotive fleet, in 1891 two further locomotives were taken into stock. These were not under-powered, being two very sturdy 0-6-0 tank locomotives built by Bagnall's of Stafford, England. They were -

No.6 "St. Philip" Bagnall, no. 1308 November 1890 0-6-0T
No.7 "St. Andrew" Bagnall, no. 1310 April 1891 0-6-0T

However, close scrutiny of the works' photograph of "St. Philip" shows it carrying the works' plate 1310, with a construction date of November 1890.

They cost the company £1,393 each, and had copper fireboxes and a wheel-base of 9ft. As a result of their size, they were in reality too heavy for the line, and wreaked havoc on the ill-maintained trackwork. They were sold on after the re-gauging of the railway to the Demerara Railway of British Guiana for further service.

However, another uncertainty arises over these two locomotives. According to the records of the Demerara Railway, the latter organisation wrote asking for spares for both engines on 17 February 1889, and on 6 February 1901 for spares for 1308 only. It is possible that the earlier letter was mis-dated, but these do confirm the widely-held views on Barbados that they did go to British Guiana.

Black, Hawthorn 0-4-0ST 'St. Michael' on a contractor's train, Belle Gully bridge, 1880. (DJH)

This is the only photograph that has been traced of the Vulcan Foundry 2-6-2 tank locomotives built in 1882. (BMHS)

A works photo of Bagnall 0-6-0T no. 6 "St. Philip", which later on was passed to the Demerara Railway of British Guiana. (Allan C. Baker)

The 2' 6" Gauge Locomotives

These have been somewhat easier to trace, as there are more recent records kept of them. The entire roster was constructed by the Baldwin Locomotive Works of Philadelphia, USA. The Bridgetown and St.Andrew's Railways Ltd ordered four tank locomotives, their details being -

| No 1 | Baldwin 16269 | 1898 | 2-8-2T | "Alice" |
| No 2 | Baldwin 16270 | 1898 | 2-8-2T | "Beatrice" |

Other details of these particular locomotives included -

Cylinders:	11" x 16"
Driving wheel diameter:	30"
Steam pressure:	160 lbs
Weight on driving wheels:	47,200 lbs
Total weight:	64,950 lbs

The other locomotives built at this time were smaller, but very similar to each other, but had differing wheel arrangements. They were -

| No 3 | Baldwin 16331 | 1898 | 0-6-0T | "Catherine" |
| No 4 | Baldwin 16332 | 1898 | 2-6-0T | "Dorothy" |

Cylinders:	11" x 16"
Driving wheel diameter:	30"
Steam pressure:	160 lbs
Weight on driving wheels:	34,400 lbs
Total weight:	40,100 lbs

The only obvious difference in appearance between them was that the 2-6-0T had a longer front end, to accommodate the pony truck below.

A new No.3 was ordered from Baldwin's in 1919; as it also carried the number 3, the existing Nos.3 and 4 were renumbered, while former No.3 was converted into a 2-6-0T, to be like its

Works photos of Baldwin 0-6-0T no. 3 'Catherine' and 2-6-0T no. 4 'Dorothy' (BNT)

Works photograph of Baldwin 16269, 1898-built 2-8-2T no. 2 'Beatrice' (DB)

One of the Baldwin 2-6-0T awaiting scrapping after the closure of the line. The 0-6-0T had by this time been converted to a 2-6-0T so it is impossible to say which of the pair this is. Note the extended side tanks, loss of the cow-catchers and other modifications to boiler fittings. (BMHS)

Two trains headed by Baldwin 2-8-2T locos crossing at an unknown location - possibly Windsor. With turntables at both ends of the line, the general operation of locomotives smokebox forwards is clearly shown in this view. Only after closure north of Bathsheba were trains back to Bridgetown operated bunker first. (BNT)

sister. The locomotive roster was then -

No 1   Baldwin 16269   1898   2-8-2T   "Alice"
No 2   Baldwin 16270   1898   2-8-2T   "Beatrice"
No 3   Baldwin 52196   1920   2-8-2T   (*)
No 4   Baldwin 16331   1898   2-6-0T   "Catherine"
No 5   Baldwin 16332   1898   2-6-0T   "Dorothy"

(* name, if any, unknown).

The line ran with this fleet until its demise. However, most of the locomotives were not serviceable by 1937 in any event, although all bar no.3 were re-boilered in 1916/17 (except no.5, which received its new boiler in 1922/23).

They were all coal-fired, but were converted to oil-firing in 1922, after the arrival of the new No.3. They were also all fitted with Westinghouse air brakes, but that equipment fell out of use as time passed, as the locomotives' braking system, along with their general condition, deteriorated. They were also all fitted with dynamos, which generated the lighting for the carriages.

The conversion to oil-firing ruined the aesthetics of the rear of the locomotives. Gone were the fluted coal-bunkers which had been in keeping with the general over-all lines of the locomotives, being replaced by angular utilitarian tanks. Some enlargements of illustrations reveal how much this altered their appearance.

They were all scrapped when the railway was closed. Indeed, Mr. Bland's report stated, "They are no longer fit for service and should be condemned forthwith". Unfortunately, they were.

An enlargement from a picture of a train in Consett's Cutting, showing the utilitarian, boxy tank fitted to Baldwin 2-8-2Ts nos. 1 and 2 in place of the original fluted and shapely coal bunkers after conversion to oil firing. (DJH)

An enlargement of a postcard of the Bridgetown station area showing the original fluted coal bunker on a Baldwin 2-6-0T. Modellers will be able to discern many other minor details of the scene by close examination of this illustration. (DJH)

The Rail Motor

Bogie Petrol Rail Motor Coach, Barbados Ry., built by the Drewry Car Co. Ltd.
(Works photograph published in 'The Locomotive' magazine of March 15th 1924).

About 1926, the railway acquired a rail motor intended for running inexpensive excursions. This was a single passenger coach with a cab at either end and a motor. It was built by the Baguley Company, who later became part of the Drewry Company, an English manufacturer of small diesel and petrol locomotives and railcars.

Records show that it was in fact built in 1923, Baguley works number 1326, its motor rated at 60HP.

It was reported in detail in the contemporary English railway press, and generally hailed as a notable advance in internal combustion motive power. If only it had been.

It was constructed with a steel chassis and frames, and a wooden superstructure. Designed with tropical use in mind, it had a double roof to allow for coolness inside its passenger saloons and louvered wooden shades to its windows. Described as having "a neat and excellent appearance", one could wonder why, for although the wooden body was as so described, the whole effect was somewhat negated by the railcar's corrugated upper roof, which gave the car the appearance having a roof off a tin shed!

It had a seating capacity of forty-four. These were accommodated in a first-class saloon for nine passengers, and in a thirty-

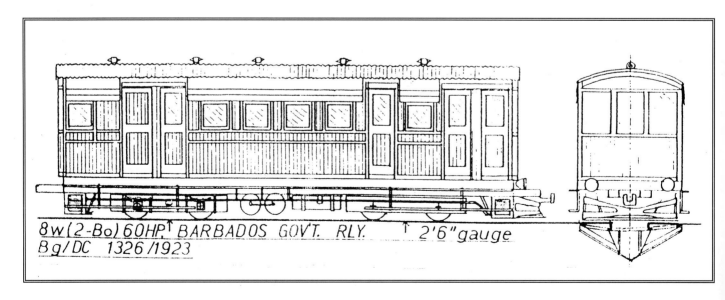

The Barbados Railway Rail Motor drawn to OO scale (1:76) for modellers by Mr. S.H. Coulson,
reproduced with his kind permission, courtesy of the 009 Society.

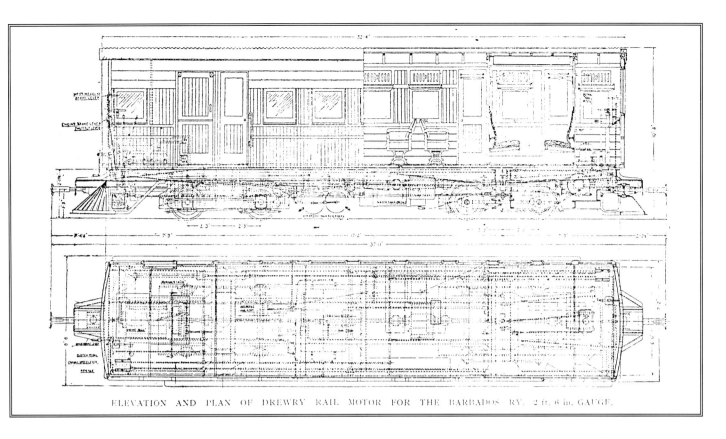

Elevation and plan of the Drewry Rail Motor, as published in 'The Locomotive' magazine, March 15th 1924.

five seat saloon for third-class travellers. Access to the first-class compartment was by an end door, and the third-class accommodation had side doors into the one long saloon. The railcar also contained a small luggage compartment between the third-class saloon and one of the driving cabs.

The bodywork and internal fittings were described as follows:-

"The windows are fitted with louvre frames and smoked glass, and also strong blinds of leather faced cloth. The inside of the coach is panelled with Venesta, the matchboarding and bodyframes being of teak, varnished inside and out".

Much was made of the car's technical design and features. It had a four-cylinder petrol engine, 5½in. diameter by 6in. stroke, developing 60-65 brake horse-power at 1000rpm. It had a three-speed gear box, allowing four mph in first, ten mph in second, and 15 mph in top gear. Its performance was hampered by this lack of power and speed - although at the time of manufacture, this was not realised. This all resulted in a grossly under-powered, low performance vehicle.

Other technical features made much of included -
Westinghouse air brakes, driven from an axle-driven compressor.
Manually-operated screw brakes, operated from either cab.
Sanding gear (again operable from both ends of the car).
A 30-gallon water tank.
A 60-gallon petrol tank.
Electric searchlights at each end of the car, which could display a white or red light (depending on direction).
Electric internal lighting.
Emergency oil lamps.
Extensive tool boxes at each end of the car.

It was claimed that the car was capable of ascending a 1 in 28

gradient on a 250ft. radius curve at a speed of five mph. Towing a trailer, it was claimed, only reduced the speed to an ascent at four mph. Despite the gear/speed ratios referred to above, the car was alleged to be able to cruise on level track at 18 mph.

The chassis of the railcar was tested on the Leek and Manifold Light Railway, in Staffordshire, England. Supposedly loaded to allow for the (then absent) bodyweight, it performed most satisfactorily on this sharply-curved 2ft 6in-gauge line. Again, much was played of its colonial potential, and its trials in Staffordshire. A party of engineers from the British, Colonial and Indian Railways attended the trials and expressed themselves pleased with the performance.

The Barbados Railway authorities were not, however. It is reported that on its inaugural trial run, the railcar ran out as far as Bathsheba, but on the return, failed to surmount Consett's Cutting, and had to be rescued by a steam loco. This single incident immediately condemned the vehicle in the eyes of the railway management, and it was doomed from then on. Its use in Barbados therefore seems to have been fairly unsuccessful. Its Westinghouse brakes were a type of brake unfamiliar to its Barbadian driver, who allegedly disconnected them, thus relying on its manual brakes only. It did survive, however, until the end of the railway's existence, though by then it had long since lost its motor. It was advertised for sale, on the close of the railway, as -

"Coach. 16 tons. Original M.Coach. Engine out. Serviceable"

There were also two inspection trolleys available for use. A photo in the Baldwin Magazine, showing the front end of one on shed in the roundhouse, suggests that it was similar in concept to the American "Galloping Goose" railcars.

The Rolling Stock

There appear to be no official records kept of the rolling stock. By deduction, and a little assumption in some cases, the following information has been discovered about it.

Passenger coaches

Originally, the passenger stock was four-wheeled, but was converted to bogie stock on re-gauging in 1898. No record has yet come to light as to their manufacturer, for the opening of the line in 1881. They appear on contemporary photographs from 3ft 6in-gauge days, and, so far, all photos show up to four carriages.

They were open-balconied, with a raised, clerestory roof and matchboard sides. They had 16 windows per side arranged in groups of two, the windows being considerably larger in depth than those on the subsequent 2ft 6in ones.

Records suggest that, initially, there was the following passenger rolling stock:

One single first-class coach, seating 16 passengers.
Two mixed-class coaches, seating 16 first- and 24 third-class passengers.
It is possible that the fourth coach was an additional third-class coach, seating 48 passengers
There was also a short, four-wheeled guard's van, which, at one end of its body, had lookouts on each side.

The third-class accommodation had wooden seats, reputedly running the length of the carriages along their sides, while the more luxurious first-class carriages had plush velvet seats. It is reported that there were always considerably more passengers travelling in the third-class carriages than in the more expensive accommodation!

Subsequent reports about the railway's 3ft 6in-gauge stock suggest that there were in fact -
Four composite 1st/2nd-class carriages
Five third-class carriages
- but this does not tally with other information regarding the passenger rolling stock.

Later 2ft 6in-era photographs show clearly that there were some carriages quite different from the remainder. These were from the earlier era and appeared shorter (in length), taller and wider.

It is thought that there were four of these later coaches, built for the 2ft 6in era, which were longer, with different roofs, body styles and which were on under-frames clearly designed for bogies. Their sides had deep sunshades, with much shallower windows - more appropriate perhaps in the Caribbean climate than the earlier coaches. Photos show at least some of this later build had fourteen windows along their sides, arranged in groups of two.

By the 1930s, the livery was described as "drab", i.e. a mid-brown colour. From all accounts, however, the paint colour was entirely academic, as the coaching stock was usually in need of a thorough repainting, which it never received. Photographs dating back to the wider-gauge days suggest that a much lighter livery was then used, but, as only monochrome photographs exist, one can only speculate as to their actual colour. Certainly they were of a more ornate livery, clearly stating the class of carriage in words above the windows, and the company's crest displayed

Church Lads' Brigade photo of 1903, taken when they were assembled at Bridgetown station before going on the train. The carriage immediately behind them is a former 3'6" gauge one - see page 12 for lower body details of this type of coach.
(Walter Parkinson, courtesy of BNT)

prominently below.

In her memoirs, the daughter of Walter Merrivale, Attorney and Managing Director of the original company, wrote of the double-deck car (which later was used by the ex-contractors' locomotive, St. Michael, on the local service into Bridgetown):

"Father also built a special railway car for us. It had three compartments downstairs and an upstairs like an old-fashioned bus. In this we used to travel with the cats and monkey complete. If a hat blew off, the train was stopped, and a negro sent back for it".

Passenger Rolling Stock List

Company No.	Class	Capacity	Weight	Comments
1	1st	16	8 tons	originally 3ft 6in gauge.
2	3rd	46?	8 tons	originally 3ft 6in gauge.
3	composite	16 1st/24 3rd	10 tons	originally 3ft 6in gauge.
4	3rd	50	10 tons	new for 2ft 6in gauge.
5	3rd	50	10 tons	new for 2ft 6in gauge.
6	3rd	50	10 tons	new for 2ft 6in gauge.
7	3rd	50	10 tons	new for 2ft 6in gauge.
8	composite	16 1st/24 3rd	10 tons	originally 3ft 6in gauge.
9	4-wh.manager's car	-	3 tons?	
10	bogie goods van	-	8 tons	
11	4-wh.goods van (56*)-		5 tons	
141	open bogie stock*	65-70 3rd	15 tons?	
143	open bogie stock*	65-70 3rd	15 tons?	
144	open bogie stock*	65-70 3rd	15 tons?	
146	open bogie stock*	65-70 3rd	15 tons?	

*These are from the freight stock roster.
No.56 is a converted freight van.
Nos.141, 143, 144 and 146 are bogie open wagons, converted into "excursion wagons" of which two were held in reserve. At least two are reported to have had some form of roof fitted during their days as excursion stock, and a relatively recent greetings card clearly showed one of them in a train.

There were discrepancies in the contemporary reported statistics of rolling stock, depending on which list was consulted. In the above list, the carriage weights are from the inventory of rolling stock for disposal in 1937. They may conflict with other information.

A scene on the east coast, possibly at Bathsheba, showing freight wagons being used for passengers on an excursion train. (BMHS)

Barbados Railway 2'6" gauge 3rd class bogie coach. (MK)

Blow-up of the wagon loaded with barrels at Bath. (DJH)

Freight Stock

Mr. Gilling's report details the following information about the freight stock. It will be noted that there are duplicate numbers in the lists, which apparently Mr. Gilling compiled with some difficulty.

Mr. Gilling reported, "As there is no record book of Rolling Stock or Plant it has been a lengthy and tedious process to analyse and classify the various vehicles...".

The article in the Baldwin Magazine mentions the delivery of 30 new freight wagons in 1919. No details have emerged as to which these were.

A further delivery of eight-ton wagons took place in 1928/9.

Freight Rolling Stock List

Class	Numbers in stock	Capacity (Tons)	Inside Dimensions	Design	Use
A	18	7	14'0" x 7'0"	high sides	sugar, stone, sand and bales
AA	31	8	15'0" x 6'9"	high sides	cases and general merchandise
B	2	6	13'0" x 6'0"	low sides	rum, sugar, ballast, general merchandise
C	10	6	14'0" x 7'0"	low sides	
D	4	8	14'0" x 7'6"	low sides	
E	2	15	37'3" x 8'0"	platform	rails, timber, machinery etc.
AA converted	4	6	14'0" x 7'0"	various	
B converted	5	6	13'9" x 6'9"	various	
C converted	4	6	14' 0" x 7'0"	various	
D converted	3	6	14'0" x 7'6"	various	cane traffic
BK converted	2	6	15'3" x 6'7"		
BP converted	6	6	15'3" x 6'7"		

Stock numbers:

A   21, 24, 25 (not recommended for service)
AA   26, 27*, 28, 30, 32, 35, 38, 40, 43, 45, 46, 49,
       50, 51, 52, 53, 54, 55-83 (not 73 & 78)
B   73*, 78
C   102-107, 111-114
D   123, 124, 132, 134
E   142, 145
D   135 (travelling oil tank)

*at workshops for general repairs

Cane wagons:

AA   29, 33, 34, 36, 41, 42, 44, 47, 48#
B   74, 77, 79, 80, 81, 82
BK   84, 86
BP   93-98
C   101, 109, 115, 116
D   128, 131, 133

#derailed with canes on 10 February 1934.

Wagons at Bridgetown Station - see also the $1 stamp on the rear cover (BNT)

Some Spoken Recollections of the Line
by Dorothy de C. Boyce (née Horsford) (recorded by the Author, 1987)

When I was a girl, there used to be a railway line with a puffing train. Fairchild Street (where there is now a market) was, in the beginning, the railway station of that small railway line. It used to come in from Bathsheba in the morning, and go out again in the evening, about half past four. People working in town used to hurry, shops shut at four, so everybody tried to get to the railway station and get on the train by half past four.

It was Half a Crown to Bathsheba. I don't know how much it was to other places; I only ever used it to Bathsheba. But you started off, and you headed through Fairfield. You passed by Windsor and Three Houses and you came to Consett's Cutting, which was a bit of a slope and it used to go pup, pup, pup, struggling up the hill. Once on the way, it was wet and they had to get help. Another engine push and one pull, or whatever. Then it went by Consett Bay, by Bath, it went around the coastline by Tent's Bay, and on to Bathsheba station. There it stopped, the people from that end of Bathsheba got out there.

A group of young ladies at Bathseheba in the 1920s. The three girls in hats are some of the Horsford sisters - Hester, Dorothy (the author of this section), and Beryl.
(DRH)

After a few minutes it came on, up around by Powell Springs, and it used to stop in front of Powell Springs too. So if we were down there, we didn't get off at the station, we went right to Powell Springs in it. Because right in front of Powell Springs was a tank with a hose, and they would stop there and fill up with water and we children would climb all over the hose and be in everybody's way while the poor men were trying to fill it.

But they all knew us well, because we were down there for three months. So, day in day out, they saw all of us little Horsfords. They got to know our names and chatted with us. As a matter of fact, if you had a list, sort of bicarb, you know, salts, newspaper, toothpaste, biscuits, condensed milk - whatever you wanted - you just gave the list to the conductor (or whatever you call him) on the train; not the driver, the other man. (The guard?). The guard! You see, it's so long since I used that word, and he would buy everything and bring it back for you next morning.

So, off it went again, right on past Cattlewash, down around Chalky Mount, right along to Belleplaine where it turned around. But it didn't come back down then, it spent the night and it came up in the morning.

Around seven, or somewhere there, you'd here the train coming (toot!) around Tenby Point. Everybody'd get ready and run down the line. All the people who had to go to work or go into town on business had to use the train because there were no buses then. You had either to take the train, or a buggy and horse, or something. So the train would slow down and stop wherever it saw people running and picked you up. It didn't bother about the station. They knew all who was going to do business in town

and they stopped for you. And off you'd go…

Once in a way we used to get a trolley. We had to go and ask the Stationmaster to lend us a trolley and all of us children would push it and jump on it. They had a kind that you'd push backwards and forwards, or they had a kind that you'd just run and jump on it. There was a little bit of a slope down by Cattlewash, and there you could get a ride for nearly a mile, all the way. And that's where we used to have best time. Then we had to push it all the way back, the whole lot of us taking turns, two sitting down, three pushing, change round.

Moonlight nights we'd used to get two trolleys, collect all the children, take some lemonade and sweet biscuits, and soon be having a party. We'd go down the line to an empty part and have a picnic big-times.

As a matter of fact, in those days, in a house down at Bathsheba, which is now called Ruby, there lived a funny old woman called Mrs Swain. She used to tell fortunes. And she had a house fixed up. She had a bead curtain hanging over the door. She used to feed her fowls on the veranda, so all the time you were walking about, chickens were in and out between your feet. But we'd use to go there, and Mrs Swain would tell us fortunes. You had to cross her hand with silver, so we'd ask Mother for Half a Crown, because that's the biggest silver coin we had in those days, we didn't have Crowns out here, we had only Half-Crowns.

Mrs Swain would take some dirty old greasy cards. We declared she fixed her hair with castor oil because she always smelt of caster oil, and she had coloured bead strings hanging around her neck and bangles on her arm that went jingle jangle all the time she's telling the fortune. We were a little afraid of her,

Powell Spring Hotel, Bathsheba, with the now lifted railway line immediately adjacent. (DJH)

POWELL SPRING HOTEL

EARBADOS   B.W.I.

because we thought she could work magic.

Anyway, she'd take out the cards, and tell you to cut, and cut again. Then she would start putting them out. This one means that you'd be going on a journey, that one means you'd be going to get married twice. This one means that you're going to do well at school, that one means something else… All way going… Then she would tell us of some misfortune, boy, we were so afraid when we came out. Each of us went in alone, you were not allowed to have anybody with you. We came out trembling, all the way going home saying "What did Mrs Swain tell you? What did Mrs Swain tell you - true? You'd better hadn't tell Mother, huh, and so we would enjoy Mrs Swain. Never went to stay at Bathsheba without going two or three times to Mrs Swain's house. It was a big event.

Well, the house, Powell Springs we stayed in. Daddy and Mother had it every year for many years when we were growing up; I wouldn't like to say how many, about eight or nine, something so. We had no electric light; we had kerosene oil lights. We had to light them, and put them in a glass box because the wind would blow them out. We had no water; there was a spring running behind, and every morning, the servants would go and bring three or four buckets of water into a kind of tub thing, and later in the day they'd fill it up again. For the whole three months we were at Bathsheba, we never had a bath! We went in the sea three times a day, but we never saw a freshwater bath the whole time, never. Because they used the water to drink, and the water to cook, and perhaps if you had a little a bit you could wash your face, but it was scarce, and Mother would say "Leave that water

alone!" We couldn't take water to wash shells; (we) had to go down and get a bucket of sea water and come back. So, those were the days when young people enjoyed themselves. We had no television, no radio, no nothing. Shells to play with and each other to chase, we never even heard about drugs, never! We didn't even know what was divorce, much less anything else.

So, Jimmy wants me to talk, well he's getting a dose of it, so serve him jolly well right. I don't think I can say anything else. We used to like the train, we used to hear it whistle. We all run out to watch it and wave to it, but, in a couple of minutes, slowly chug, chug, chug, she went by. No more train until tomorrow. Well, that's how it was.

I have been in the train three or four times. Little small seats, you could sit two, with a little aisle next to it. I remember hear-

Bathsheba, 1920s, A view of the resort showing the traditional 'colonial' style buildings, with the railway running through the village. (DRH)

ing that somebody's hat blew off; they made a fuss, and the train stopped and let her go back and pick up her hat (that's a fact, that's not a tarry-diddle). Another thing, a girl that I knew, put her head out once to look at something, and it was taken off. Well, they were going through a culvert thing or whatever; she got a lash and was killed, in the train, so…

(What did the locomotives run on, coal or bagass?).

Coal not bagass, no, no, no, not bagass. Coal or wood, not bagass. Well, they took water, so they created steam, and they had a fire, because they had a stoking fireman and to tell you the honest truth, Jimmy, I never looked to see.

(Where did they catch the water? Can you remember where it stopped for water?).

About three places in all. They stopped for water outside Powell Springs where we lived. Then there was another one along down the East Coast Road, so if they were taken short earlier, they had to stop there. It was a big round… (tank?), yes, and a hose. All they did was put the hose in the thing and turn on something, that's all. There was fresh water in there, you see, so there must have been a tap up to supply it with water, but it had the height, so it would run down into the…the tank was about the height of that picture there.

(And there was one there at Powell Springs?).

In front of Powell Springs there was one, right there; but there were others along the line. I didn't particularly take note where, because that's the one I know, but I have seen going along in the trolley, all the way down towards Belleplaine. Maybe we used to go quite as far as Chalky Mount, on the trolleys you know, because we just kept going, as long as we liked, we had it. But there were a frame with a tank down towards Chalky Mount way.

It used to turn round at Belleplaine, on a turntable I believe, so they say. I never particularly noticed that, or went to look at the turntable, but I knew it was there.

(And there was another one at Bridgetown?).

Something must have turned, or it shunted into…they must have had a way of turning round in Bridgetown. I never thought about that, either!

(It carried the sugar cane?).

It carried the finished sugar, it carried barrels and barrels of…just now, what do you call the thing, syrup (molasses, sort of thing?); molasses and syrup. There's something called fancy molasses, which was treacle; in England it would be treacle. It's before it's finished into the sugar; you got big puncheons of that because, that was exported away. It was used in making biscuits, so Huntley & Palmer and so, would buy that kind of treacle, mixed in ginger biscuits that they manufactured and so. A lot of it used to go abroad.

(The trains went through all the canefields past the factories and so?).

One trainline through, only. So it didn't go in any other, so it would have been no use to take canes (raw canes?), no.

(So it only carried the finished products?).

Right. Mind you, it brought up things for the canes, like manure, and parts of engines or loads of puncheons, the stakes, things like that. But to pile the canes in, I never, never, never saw that.

(What happened to all the freight when it got to Bridgetown station?).

Well, it was unloaded, on a siding there, and I seem to remember men. Mind you, they had horse-drawn carts, mule-drawn flat carts, open. A horse between two sharves, and a man sat in the front, and they would pile each cart with bags or barrels, or what it had in it. And those horse carts, mule carts and men running with carts, transported it from the railway station across and to the side of the wharves, put it into lighters. Lighters, when they were full, big lighters, pushed off, and with men running on the side with oars, they got it out, alongside the ships in Carlisle Bay. The ships swung it up in a net by a crane or whatever, and put it down in the hold.

And when the lighter was empty, it went back in, got another full whatever, and there was two to three hundred lighters, all about up in the harbour and everywhere. Each company had its own lighters, like Mussons & Company, or Jason Jones or Da Costa's had a hundred lighters. Each company had their own and they took the cargo for their own line in their own lighters. Harrison lighters didn't carry cane for Da Costa or sugar or whatever. Each had their own lighters and their own lightermen.

Now I understand that, in 1937, the railway was closed down. There were lots of reasons really. The line was always having to be renewed, because it passed through a very salty district, which ate away the metal line. But that was not the only reason. Buses had arrived, and were taking people all around, and trucks. Each estate had their own trucks, so they were loaded up and carried their own sugar and fancy molasses and so, into Bridgetown direct without having to cart it to a railway line. It was quicker and easier, so gradually, transport really finished off the railway, so it was no longer needed. People had motor cars. A lot of people who had taken the train to go here and there, were now beginning to get the early motor cars, so, once more, motor traffic really killed the railway.

(Can you tell me something about the mule trams in Bridgetown?).

Honestly, Jimmy, you're not satisfied with making me talk about the old train; now you're asking me about the mule trams? You really don't know what to do. Anyway, I did travel on the mule trams, quite often, and I enjoyed it very much. It was a lot of fun, it was open on all sides, it was just a row of seats, five or so, and two nice, big, Kentucky mules pulled it.

It started in Bridgetown in what was known as The Green, in front of the public buildings. One line went up through Broad

Mrs. Agnes Horsford, her daughter Gwen and friends trolley-riding, Bathsheba, 1920s. (BMHS)

Street, up to Barbary's Hill. One line went to Fontabelle and one line came up Bay Street, right out in front of the rocks where we live, right on to St.Lawrence.

It stopped at St.Lawrence corner, and the man got out and turned the backs of the seats round to the other side to make it look the other way. The man standing in the front, who I suppose you call the driver, he had a sticking up stick he used to turn round and round to use as a brake.

When they were coming up Garrison Hill, two mules couldn't pull the tram when it was full, or so, so they had to hitch on another mule to give a little help up Garrison Hill. And, when they got to the top, it stopped, and unhitched that mule and carried it back down to the bottom to wait for the next tram.

A Sunday afternoon outing was to take the tram from The Garrison, where I used to live with Auntie Floss quite often, and drive up to St.Lawrence. Get out and walk down by the sea and the beach, and stroll around a little bit, and take another tram back down to the Garrison. We'd had a lovely afternoon's outing.

I only think it must have been about threepence to drive that distance by the tram, because it was a shilling all the way into town.

I told Jimmy that I remember, when I was in Bridgetown, waiting for the trams to start, because if I was going up to Auntie May, or going back to Auntie Floss's from town, all the trams went from the same place. I would go there and stand up and wait there for the tram I wanted. If the (Public) Buildings' clock chimed, the hour, or the quarter, or the half, off started the mules, they only had to hear the chimes, they knew it was time. If the driver was standing talking, and he hadn't locked off the brake good, the mule start pulling off, and he had to run behind, calling whoa, whoa, and jump on, and run down and catch the reins up! We used to think that was lovely.

Well, the tram station (depot) was just at the foot of Garrison Hill, right in front of where is now the Electric Company, and the building now used by the Electric Company was the offices of the mule tram company.

Oh, the trams and so were in this area; opposite in a kind of hangar thing - sheds I suppose you'd call them - and the mule stalls were there too. So, I was very sorry when they finally finished up, 'cos I thought they were a lot of fun.

With the coming of motor cars, and motor transport and motor everything, Trinidad had electric trams, before the motor cars. They had electric trams running with an overhead line and a kind of a stick going up, touching it, and with the coming of the motor car, that folded down too. So, all the old things pass away, that's how it is.

Extract from "The Book of the West Indies" Edited by Francis Dodsworth, 1904

Bridgetown to Bathsheba

The climate of the tropics at five o'clock in the morning is full of deceit. There is a sweet coolness, a seductive gentleness and a luring softness - I had almost said a caress - in the air which would lead the unsuspecting tourist to suppose that the atmosphere bordered upon the confines of heaven. If for a moment he can forget the glaring sun, the dry dust, the choking apathy of mid-day, he will draw comparisons with England by no means to the credit of his own country.

When we drove through Bridgetown everything was at its best. The freshness of the morning had not yet changed into garish day. The town, though half asleep, already showed activity, yet not bustle, signs of labour but no insistent work. Bridgetown lay like a toy town, and we were not surprised to find as an unnecessary complement, a toy railway. The only thing of any size or dimensions about the Barbados Railway is the noise which it creates. Such hooting, such shrieking, such agonised howling, such painful cries, were never put forth by the Flying Dutchman or the Scotch Express. The tiny absurd engine running on a small gauge, was unable to possess its soul in patience until all the world within a radius of a mile had not only been made aware of its existence but had become fully cognisant of its importance.

Although important, the Barbados Railway can be obliging at times, and the best evidence of this is the following extract, which is taken from its own notice board: - "The ordinary trains may stop (1) to set down passengers on their informing the guard, and to take up any passengers who are then waiting there, if there is any room in the train, but the company will not be responsible for conveyance of any passenger who may fail to attract the attention of the driver or guard in time to stop the train, and to reserve the right to run any of the ordinary trains past these places without stopping". Attention, dignity, diffidence are all perfectly blended. Should the wandering passenger fail to attract the attention he may be left behind; but the railway are careful enough to point out that the error will be his, and the inward meaning of the phrase, "in time to stop the train", verges, I am inclined to believe, on the elastic.

With much puffing, shrieking, and banging of doors we crawled out of Bridgetown. Beyond a few prosperous houses and a gaunt, forbidding-looking prison, we saw nothing of interest whatever. As we left the town behind and entered into the comparative country (for in Barbados one must not forget that there are over 1,000 people to each mile, and the waste places, if not always made fertile, are invariably inhabited), we saw sugar, sugar, and still eternal sugar. On all sides the vivid green of the young sugar met our eyes, and the only change from the dull gray of the chimneys and buildings was the occasionally glaring red of the flamboyant [tree], while a few bananas, which had the appearance of having lost their way, radiated the same eternal shade of green. Wind-mills there were, cresting gentle slopes, factory chimneys stood out against the sky, and everywhere and in all places, huts. Huts small, mean, and to the casual observer insanitary, but - huts.

Slowly and with hideous noise we rattled through the country, meeting a general monotony of scenery, tempered with an atmosphere of assiduous industry. The children dispensed with clothes. The women were in thin short skirts, and displayed no diffidence about showing their legs. Even a man, probably a "lord of

Bridgetown Station, with a train headed by one of the Baldwin 2-8-2 tank locomotives. (DJH)

A postcard view of the line running beside the coast at Bathsheba. (DJH)

BATHSHEBA COAST. BARBADOS.

creation," was content to meet the world clad in a sack, by no means too long for him or for decency: and yet, with all this there was a quaint old-fashioned air about the landscape.

After a few miles the sea added colour and picturesque-ness to the scene. The flat greenness of the sugar plantations began to give way with reluctance to small hills, of which not a few were surmounted by churches; and in time, growing bolder, the landscape breaking away, became quietly aggressive, and a succession of small cliffs running down to the sea formed a welcome change to the incessant flatness of the earlier part of the journey.

Even the sea caught the infection. Small waves, called, in this part of the world "breakers," came rolling in with all the majesty and all the force with which the Atlantic dashes against the giant caves or the rough harshness of the east [?] coast of Ireland. Rocks grotesquely shaped, worn by the sea, stood out in the water, and we became aware of the startling absence of cultivation. In some measure the scenery recalled the north-east coast of Yorkshire, reconstructed upon a very, very small scale. The same bleak cliffs, the same barren air, with just a suggestion, and no more, of the wild, cold breezes of the North Sea. The same short, thin, close-cropped turfs, the same indented ragged openings in the cliffs.

With a jerk and with unnecessary fuss, which is characteristic of the railway of Barbados, we stopped at Bathsheba. We found ourselves at what the people of the place pompously call a "health resort," and if the word should suggest to the English reader something in the nature of Brighton, Worthing, Torquay or Bournemouth, and if he should find, and be shocked by the finding, that Bathsheba was a collection of small houses, smaller huts, and two dormant hotels, the scenery and climate will go far to console him.

The place provides rest, quiet and calm. In the constant, never-fading roar of the sea the visitor will find a dreamy comfort. If he looks back towards the land, the scenery, though minute, is picturesque, and even, in a quiet way, beautiful. He will realise

why the people of Barbados take a pride in Bathsheba, and he will cease to rail at the self-sufficiency which labels it "Our Health Resort".

It would be useless to deny that there are many places in England or on the coast of France infinitely more beautiful, infinitely more picturesque, infinitely more inviting, infinitely more to be desired, than this quaint out of the way spot in the West Indies. But needs must where circumstances have coerced, and to the man whom pleasure or pain, business or accident, or even the irresistible force of necessity, has driven to the West Indies, Bathsheba must come as a welcome change. To those who love to be by the side of the sea; to those whose brains are weary through work or weakness, to those for whom a tropical climate has no attractions; to those who desire perfect rest, coolness, and a reminiscence of the old land; to such Bathsheba will be a Godsend.

It differs but little from many villages that I could name in Devonshire, in Yorkshire, and in the south coast of Wales, but whereas in Wales, Yorkshire or Devonshire it would be the kind of thing we would expect to see, it is here the very apotheosis of the unforeseen. For this reason, therefore, if for this reason only, tourists to Barbados should not miss Bathsheba.

The journey on the railway, although it occupies one hour and a half, is full of quiet humour to those who can appreciate it, and mildly interesting to those who cannot. Once at Bathsheba, the invalid, the tired man, the person to whom sight-seeing has become a superfluity, will find themselves content. Content is its watchword, its excuse, and its banner. Hence, since the unique is always desirable, Bathsheba should and will remain a thing to be desired.

Source:
"The Book of the West Indies" Edited by Francis Dodsworth.
Published by George Routledge & Sons Limited, London, 1904

Consett's Cutting in the 2'6" gauge era. (DJH)

Appendices

Appendix 1 -
Income and Expenditure 1927-1937

Date	Revenue	Expenditure
January-March 1927 (3 months)	£4,512 9s 4d	£8,435 8s 7½d
1927-28	£11,978 4s 4d	£12,942 11s 8½d
1928-29	£11,100 19s 6	£17,917 9s 8d
1929-30	£11,249 19s 1½d	£13,285 10s 4d
1930-31	£8,341 10s 8d	£12,256 3s 5½d
1931-32	£6,527 2s 6½d	£11,227 15s 6d
1932-33	£7,783 1s 8½d	£11,163 4s 0½d
1933-34	£7,320 3s 1½d	£11,049 8s 8½d
1934-35	£2,783 14s 5d	£8,549 4s 4½d
1935-36	£1,567 15s 5d	£7,001 0s 5d
April-December 1936 (3 months)	£400 8s 7½d	£4,793 0s 3½d
Total	£76,565 8s 8d	£118,602 17s 1½d

Appendix 2
Passenger and Freight traffic 1927-1936

Year	No.of Passengers	Tonnage
1927	103,653	38,224.2.2.
1928	84,341	36,006.12.2.
1929	91,204	35,603.5.1.
1930	83,571	30,979.10.2.
1931	58,877	16,595.11.1.
1932	69,393	31,636.2.0.
1933	58,982	34,692.7.1.
1934*	6,832	24,654.6.1.
1935		11,806.19.0.
1936		1,842.5.2.

(*   Passenger traffic ended on 21 January 1934)

Appendix 3 - the Inventory of Items for Disposal After Closure - see original document overleaf.

Period postcard of the railway beside the coast at Bathsheba,
after the gauge had been converted. (DJH)

Barbados Government Railway.

Inventory of the most important items of Rolling Stock, Track, Machines, etc: for disposal.

Offers for all or any of these will be received by the Secretary, Railway Disposal Committee, P. O. Box 173, Bridgetown, up to the 30th October, 1937.

LOCOMOTIVES:—

No. 1	30 Tons.		Dismantled.
No. 2	30 ,,		Out of Commission, hole in boiler.
No. 3	30 ,,		Serviceable.
Nos. 4 & 5	20 ,, each.		,,

DETAILS:—

Locomotives:—

Nos. 1, 2, 3—30 Tons each.
Builders—Baldwin Loco: Works, Philadelphia.
Cylinders 13" x 16", Driving wheels 8 Connected.
30" Diam:, Two-wheeled Trucks front and rear.
Gauge 2' 6", Side Tanks 800 Imp: gallons.
Firebox—Copper.   Tubes (96) Brass.
    Oil fired.

General Condition:—

No. 1. Dismantled, requires a boiler
    Can be put back into service.
No. 2. Out of Commission due to a hole in tne boiler.   General
    condition fair.
No. 3. Serviceable.

Locomotives:—

Nos. 4 & 5—20 Tons each.
Builders,—Baldwin Loco: Works, Philadelphia.
Cylinders 11" x 16" Driving wheels 6 Connected.
30" Diam: Two-wheeled Truck (Front) 20" Diam:,
Gauge 2' 6", side Tanks 300 gallons.
Firebox—Copper.   Tubes (96) Brass.
    Oil fired.
Both of these Locos. are at present in service.
A limited quantity of spares in stock.

PASSENGER STOCK:—

No. 1 1st Class— 8 Tons.	Carry 24 Pass:	Good Condition.	
No. 2 ,, or 3rd— 8 ,,	,, 24	,,	,, ,,
No. 3 3rd Class—10 ,,	,, 37	,,	Dismantled.
Nos. 4, 5, 6, 7, & 8			
3rd Class—10 Tons each.	,, 50	,,	Serviceable.
No. 9 3rd Class— 3 Tons.	Inspection Car—Not Serviceable.		
Coach 16 ,,	Original M. Coach.	Serviceable.	
	Engine out.		

BRAKE VANS:—

1 Bogie	8 Tons 12 Tons.	Serviceable.	
1—4 Wheel	5 Tons 6 Tons.	,,	

GOODS STOCK:—

High side,   3.5 Tons. 8 Tons.
  39   Serviceable.
  11   In need of repair.
  10   Scrap.

Other Types.
  11   Serviceable.
  17   In need of repair.
   7   Scrap.

N.B. 1 Temporary Passenger Coach included in above.

TANKS (OIL ETC.)

1—5′ 0″ Diam. x 18′ 7″ long.

1—5′ 11″ Diam. x 10′ 0″ long.

2—8′ 6″ Diam. x 16′ 2″ high, Lucey Manufacturing Corpn., New York. Capacity 200 Brls. each.

1—8′ 0″ long x 4′ 10″ wide x 4′ 10″ deep.

1—Gasoline Tank—3′ 1½″ x 3′ 1″ x 1′ 0″.

3—Tanks (air)—1′ 3″ Diam. x 3′ 6″ long.

1—   „   —2′ 0″   „   11′ 0″ „

TANKS (WATER)

1 Bridgetown Station	....	17′ 6″ x 17′ 6″ x 4′ 6″ Deep.
1 Carrington „	....	17′ 6″ x 17′ 6″ x 4′ 6″ „
1 Bulkeley „	....	9′ 0″ x 1′ 11″ x 2′ 14″ „
1 Three Houses „	....	„ „ „ „
2 Bath „	....	„ „ „ „
2 „ (Galvanised) „	....	5′ 6″ wide x 7′ 6″ long x 2′ 0″ Deep.
1 Bathsheba „	....	9′ 0″ x 1′ 11″ x 2′ 14″.
3 St. Andrews „	....	„ „ „
		(one not in good condition).
1 Galvanised	....	6′ 3″ x 3′ 1″ x 1′ 0″.

1 Chain lifting block by
G. Gibbons & Co.   ....   4 to 6 tons.

CRANES.

2—3 Ton Cranes by Jesoop & Sons.

7—1 Ton Cranes by Ransomes & Rapier.
  (Viz:— Bridgetown, Bulkeley, Windsor, Carrington, Bushy Park, Three Houses, St. Andrews, respectively.)

1 Weigh-bridge—20 Tons, by Hinds.

3 Semi Rotary Pumps, size 2. 5. 8 (on oil tanks).
  Selson Engineering Coy. Ltd.

2 Force Pumps, 3″ bore.

Steel Girders of various sizes, from Bridges and Culverts.

2 Turn Tables, Ransomes & Rapier—27′ 8″ long each.

BATHSHEBA COAST. BARBADOS.

*Before and after closure. The impressions of the lifted sleepers are still visible in the trackbed,
which soon become used as a public footpath. The trackbed today forms one of
the local roads around Bathsheba. (upper DJH, lower DRH)*

LOCOMOTIVES INTERNATIONAL
BOOKS AND MAGAZINES

<table>
<tr><td>The St. Kitts Railway</td><td>Jim Horsford</td><td>1-900340-18-6</td></tr>
<tr><td>A Very British Railway</td><td>Paul Catchpole</td><td>1-900340-15-1</td></tr>
<tr><td>The Railways of Romania</td><td>Chris Bailey</td><td>1-900340-13-5</td></tr>
<tr><td>The Steam Locomotives of Czechoslovakia</td><td>Paul Catchpole</td><td>1-873150-14-8</td></tr>
<tr><td>East European Narrow Gauge</td><td>Keith Chester</td><td>1-873150-04-0</td></tr>
<tr><td>Forestry Railways in Hungary</td><td>Paul Engelbert</td><td>1-900340-09-7</td></tr>
<tr><td>Britain's World of Steam</td><td>Paul Catchpole</td><td>1-900340-14-3</td></tr>
<tr><td>Steam and Rail in Indonesia</td><td>Jack Rozendaal</td><td>1-900340-11-9</td></tr>
<tr><td>Steam and Rail in Slovakia</td><td>Paul Catchpole</td><td>1-900340-08-9</td></tr>
<tr><td>Steam and Rail in Germany</td><td>Various contributors</td><td>1-900340-06-2</td></tr>
<tr><td>Diesels & Electrics Special Edition No. 1</td><td>Various contributors</td><td>1-900340-16-x</td></tr>
<tr><td>Diesels & Electrics Special Edition No. 2</td><td>Various contributors</td><td>1-900340-17-8</td></tr>
<tr><td>Locomotives International Magazine</td><td>ISSN</td><td>1353-7091</td></tr>
</table>

*To see more details visit our web site at www.locomotivesinternational.co.uk
or write to us the address below.*

LOCOMOTIVES INTERNATIONAL **books and magazines are published by:
Paul Catchpole Ltd., The Haven, Trevilley Lane, St. Teath, Cornwall, PL30 3JS, Great Britain**

From Sugar Cane to Scenic Train...
The St. Kitts Railway
by Jim Horsford

Softback, 64 pages, (48 in full colour) over 130 photos, 17 track diagrams, 8 maps
ISBN 1-900340-18-6

UK Cover price £9.95

The Caribbean island of St. Kitts has been a producer of sugar since around 1640 and the 2'6" gauge railway was constructed to connect the sugar estates with a central sugar factory. The railway has used both steam and diesel locomotives over the years and even two ex-WW1 army surplus petrol locos. Recently tourist trains have been introduced using double-decker coaches hauled by 760mm gauge diesels bought from a sugar-beet line in Poland.

Jim Horsford has written a thoroughly researched history of the railway and the island's sugar factory. The route of the railway, including several branches, is described, mapped and profusely illustrated, as are the locomotives and rolling stock. Engineer Derek Horn has assisted with technical matters concerning the Sugar Corporation's fleet of diesel locomotives and Scenic Railway manager Steve Hites has contributed regarding the Scenic Train, including making available a set of drawings for the double-decker coaches.

Modellers of the narrow gauge will also find much inspiration here, including examples of the line's bridges, level crossings, and cane train loading and unloading facilities. Track plans of the loading stations and the sugar factory, and maps of branches to the port, the beach and a cable-hauled incline are provided, supported with lots of full colour photographs.

LOCOMOTIVES INTERNATIONAL books and magazines are published by:
Paul Catchpole Ltd., The Haven, Trevilley Lane, St. Teath, Cornwall, PL30 3JS, Great Britain
e-mail: editor@locomotivesinternational.co.uk ~ Web page: www.locomotivesinternational.co.uk